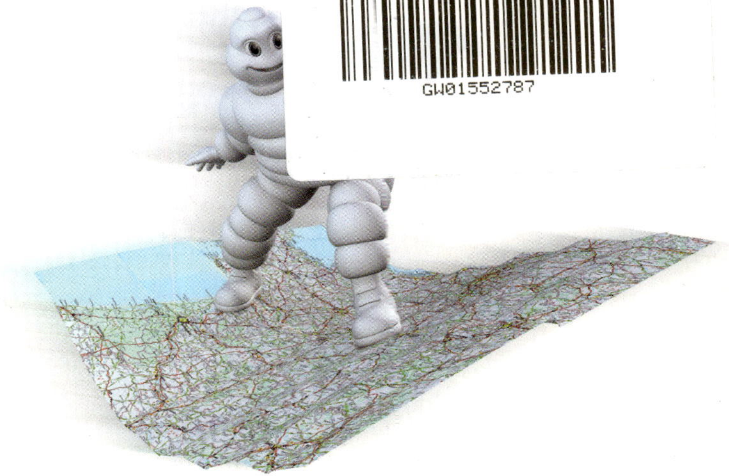

GREAT BRITAIN
& IRELAND

MOTORING ATLAS

Unitary Authorities

WALES

1. Anglesey/Sir Fôn
2. Blaenau Gwent
3. Bridgend/
   Pen-y-bont ar Ogwr
4. Caerphilly/Caerffili
5. Cardiff/Caerdydd
6. Carmarthenshire/
   Sir Gaerfyrddin
7. Ceredigion
8. Conwy
9. Denbighshire/Sir Ddinbych
10. Flintshire/Sir y Fflint
11. Gwynedd
12. Merthyr Tydfil/
    Merthyr Tudful
13. Monmouthshire/Sir Fynwy
14. Neath Port Talbot/
    Castell-nedd Phort Talbot
15. Newport/Casnewydd
16. Pembrokeshire/Sir Benfro
17. Powys
18. Rhondda Cynon Taff/
    Rhondda Cynon Taf
19. Swansea/Abertawe
20. Torfaen/Tor-faen
21. Vale of Glamorgan/
    Bro Morgannwg
22. Wrexham/Wrecsam

SCOTLAND

1. Aberdeen City
2. Aberdeenshire
3. Angus
4. Argyll and Bute
5. Clackmannanshire
6. City of Edinburgh
7. City of Glasgow
8. Dumfries and Galloway
9. Dundee City
10. East Ayrshire
11. East Dunbartonshire
12. East Lothian
13. East Renfrewshire
14. Falkirk
15. Fife
16. Highland
17. Inverclyde
18. Midlothian
19. Moray
20. North Ayrshire
21. North Lanarkshire
22. Orkney Islands
23. Perthshire and Kinross
24. Renfrewshire
25. Scottish Borders
26. Shetland Islands
27. South Ayrshire
28. South Lanarkshire
29. Stirling
30. West Dunbartonshire
31. West Lothian
32. Western Isles

Newquay

Truro

St. Ives
Hayle
Redruth
Camborne
Penryn
Penzance
St. Just
St. Michael's Mount
Sennen
Helston
Fa
Land's End

Tresco
St. Martin's
Isles of Scilly
St. Mary
Mount's Bay
St.
Lizard
Lizard Point

BRISTOL CHANNEL

Lundy

Hartland Point

Ilfracombe
Combe Martin
Lynton
Lynmouth
Croyde
Braunton
Northam
Barnstaple
Bideford
South Molton
Clovelly
Great Torrington
Kilkhampton
Winkleigh
Hatherleigh
Bude
Stratton
Holsworthy
Crediton
Tintagel
Launceston
Okehampton
EXETER
High Willhays
Moretonhampstead
Camelford
Dartmoor
Bovey Tracey
Padstow
Wadebridge
Tavistock
National
Ashburton
C O R N W A L L
Princetown
Park
Bodmin
Callington
Buckfastleigh
Fraddon
Liskeard
Saltash
Totnes
Lostwithiel
Torpoint
Plympton
St. Austell
Fowey
Looe
Modbury
Tregony
Polperro
Plymstock
Dartmouth
Mevagissey
PLYMOUTH
Newton Ferrers
Kingsbridge
St. Mawes
Salcombe
Start Point

Exmoor
Simonsbath
National

DEVON

Taw

Imouth

Keverne

Santander
Roscoff

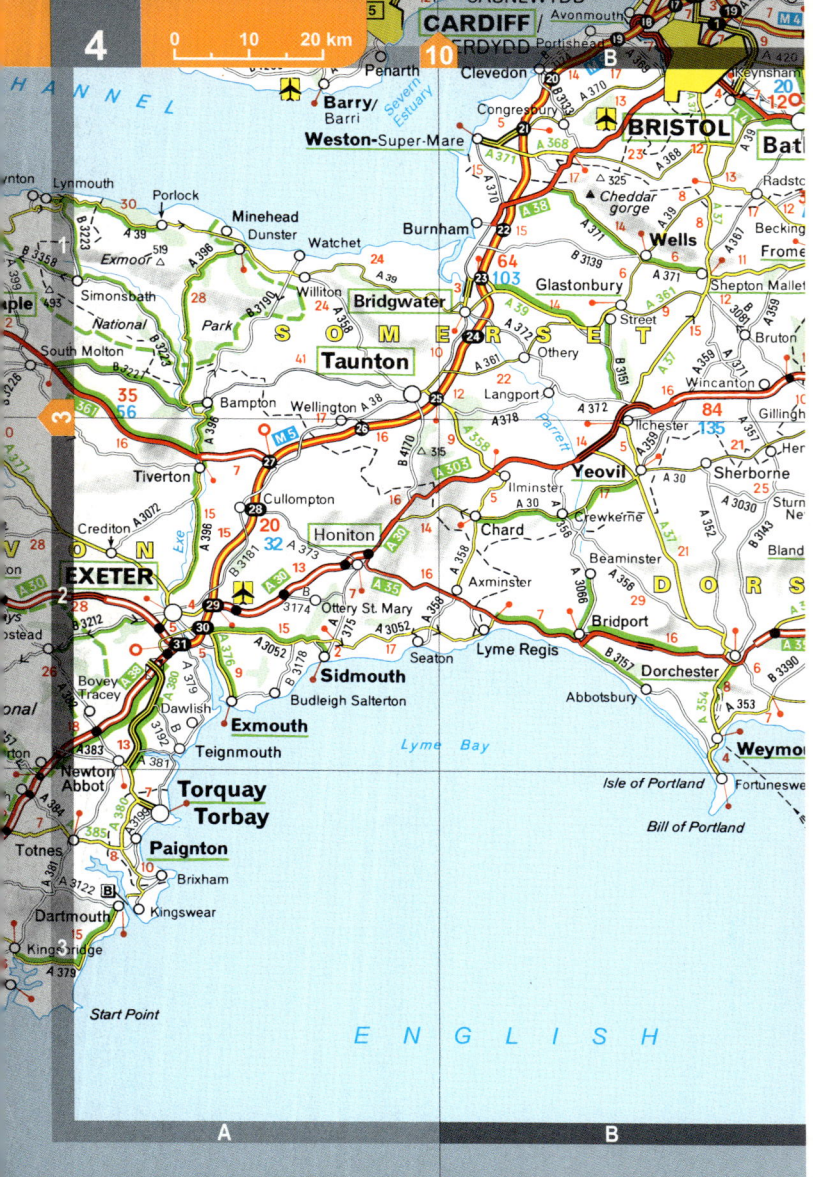

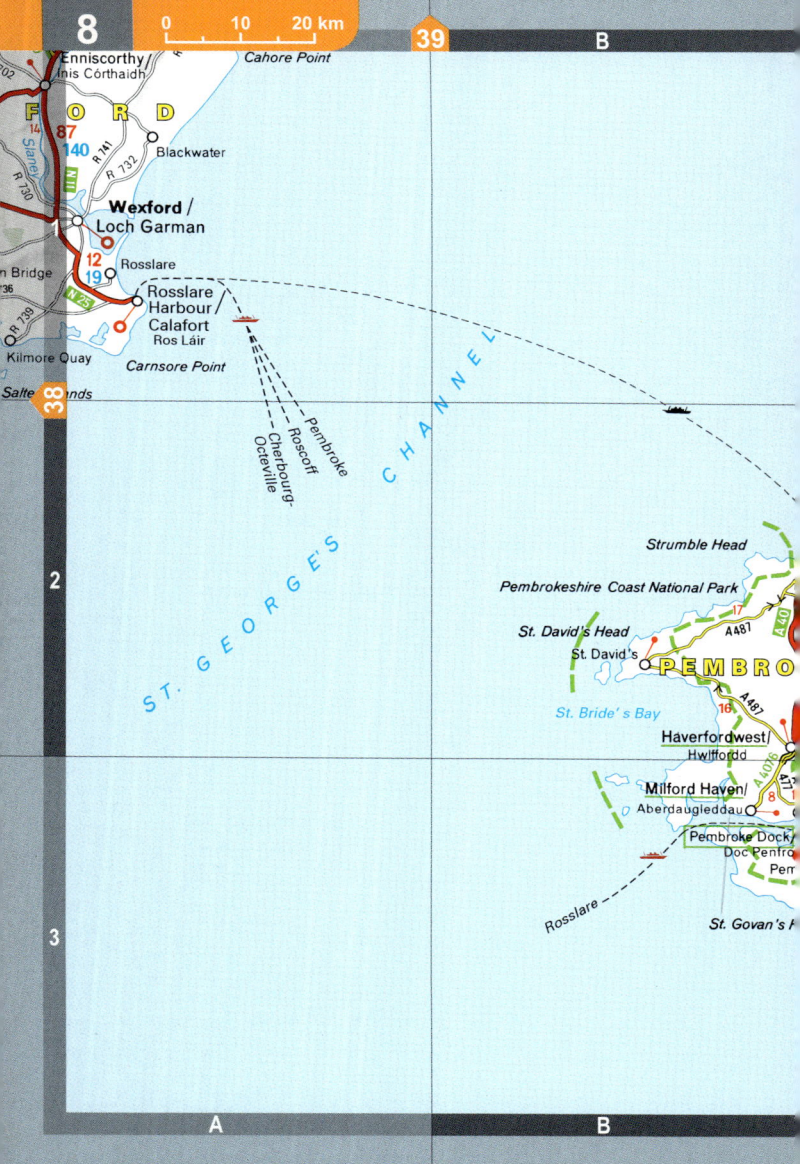

0 10 20 km

B

Cahore Point

Enniscorthy /
Inis Córthaidh

R 702

W E X F O R D

R 741

14

87

140

N 11

R 732

Blackwater

R 730

R 738

12

19

N 25

36

Wexford /
Loch Garman

Rosslare

Rosslare
Harbour /
Calafort
Ros Láir

Kilmore Quay

Carnsore Point

Salte Islands

R 739

n Bridge

38

Pembroke

Roscoff

Cherbourg-
Octeville

S T .   G E O R G E ' S   C H A N N E L

Strumble Head

Pembrokeshire Coast National Park

St. David's Head

St. David's

A 487

A 487

17

A 40

PEMBRO

2

St. Bride's Bay

16

Haverfordwest /
Hwlffordd

A 40

A 487

A 4076

Milford Haven /
Aberdaugleddau

8

1

Pembroke Dock /
Doc Penfro

Pem

Rosslare

St. Govan's

3

A B

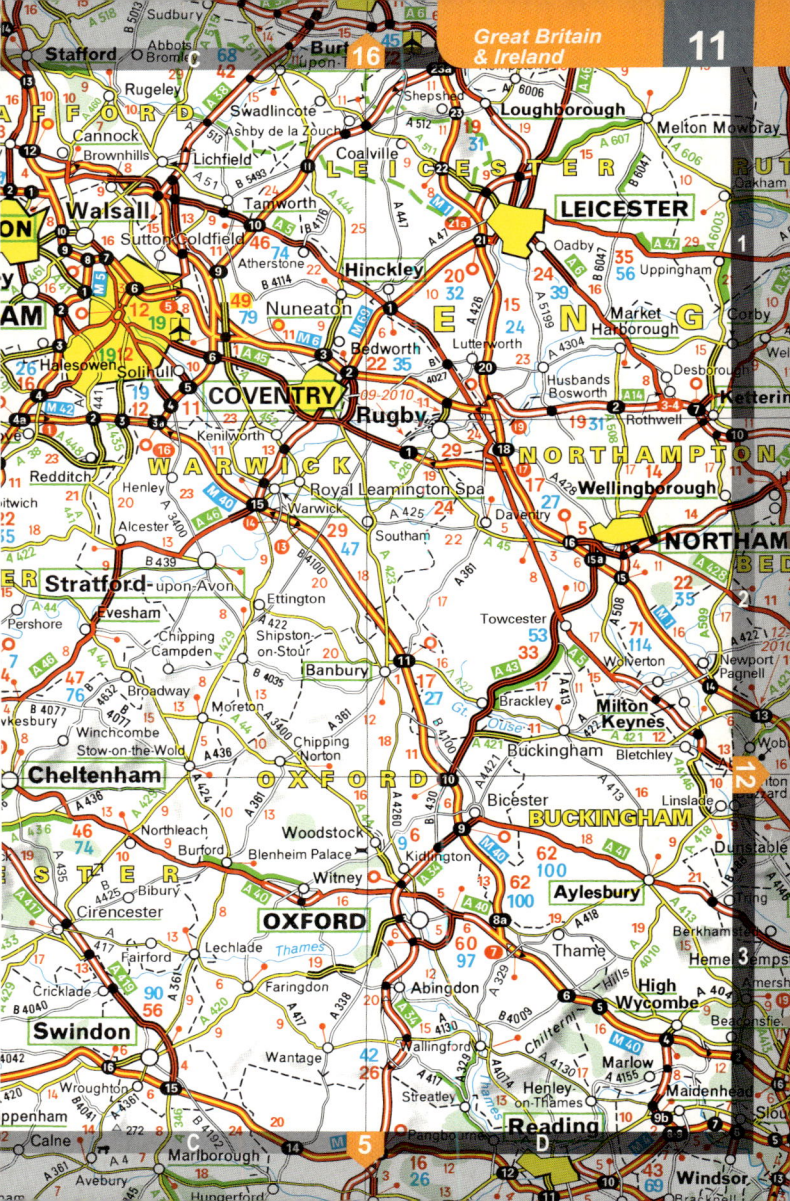

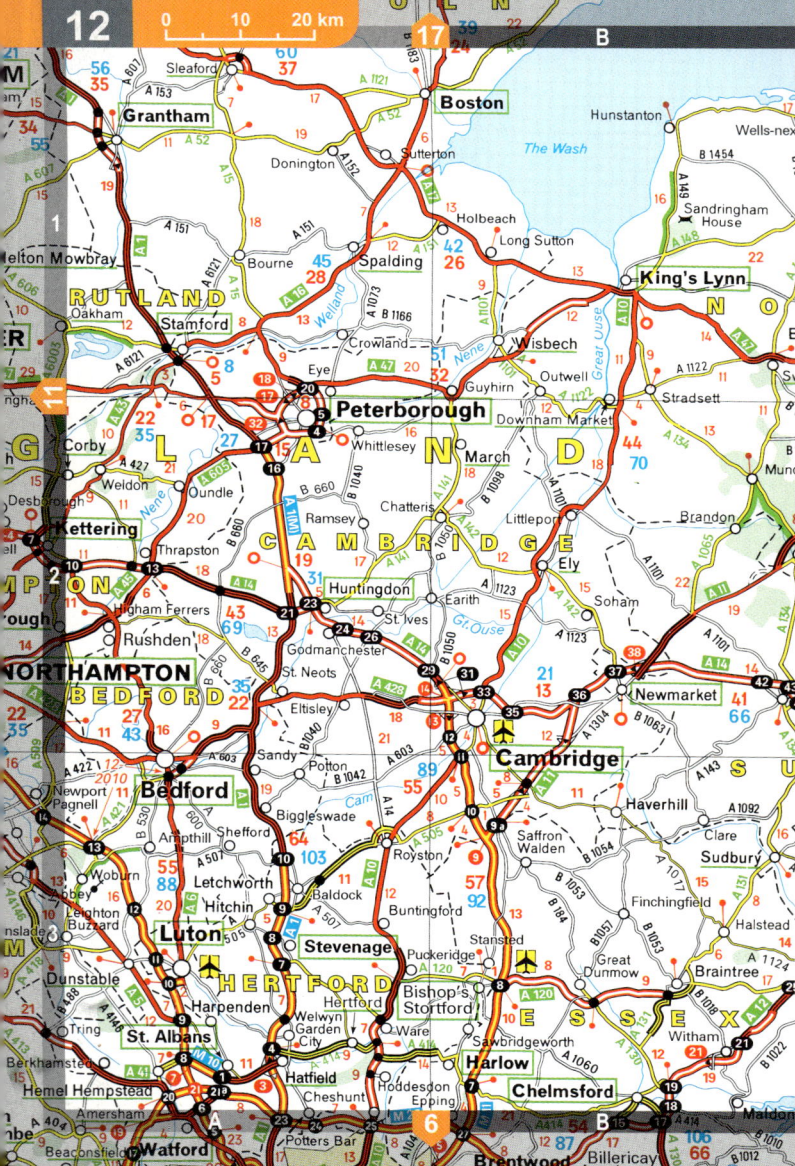

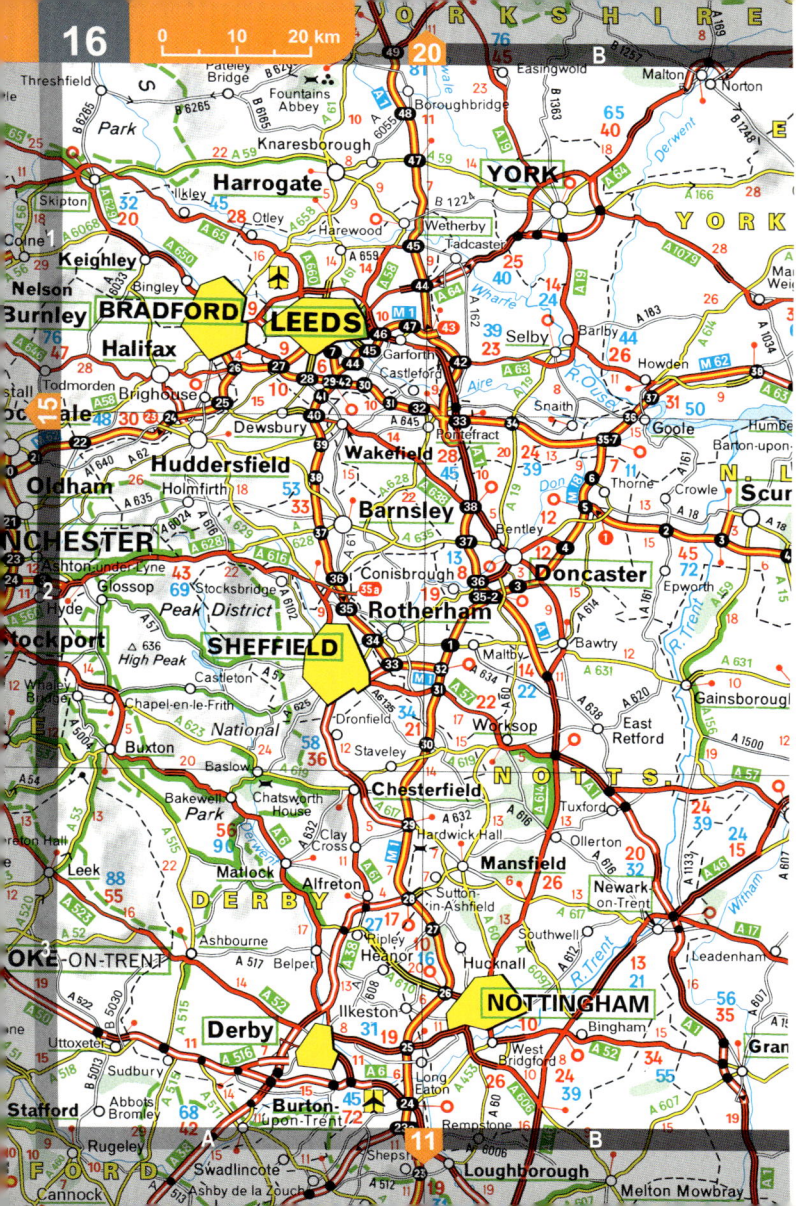

Filey
A 1039
A 64
RIDING
Wetwang
Gt. Driffield
A 614
A 164
SHIRE
A 614
Market Weighton
Leven
B 1244
A 1035
Beverley
A 164
B 1230
A 165

KINGSTON-UPON-HULL

Flamborough Head
Bridlington

Beeford
Hornsea

Hedon
B 1242
Withernsea
A 1033

River Humber
Humber Bridge
A 1077
A 1077

LINCS
nthorpe
A 160
Immingham Dock
Immingham
M 180
N.E.
Grimsby
Cleethorpes
Brigg
A 1084
Humberside
Caistor
A 46
LINCS
A 16

Patrington
Kilnsea
Spurn Head

Rotterdam
Zeebrugge

A 1103
A 631
A 631
Market Rasen
A 46
Wragby
50
31
A 153
31
50
20

Lincoln
Horncastle
Woodhall Spa
B 1188
B 1191
B 1192
B 1190

A 631
Louth
A 157
A 1031

Mablethorpe
A 1104
Sutton-on-Sea
A 1104
A 111
Alford
A 52
Partney
B 1195
Spilsby
A 155
11
18

Mablethorpe

LINCOLN
A 153
60
37
Sleaford
A 1121
A 153
A 16
39
24
B 1183
22
A 52

A 158 **Skegness**

ntham
A 52
Donington
A 152
Sutterton
A 15
A 17
A 151
Holbeach
Long Sutton
Bourne
A 151
45
Spalding
A 16
42
26
A 151

Boston

Hunstanton
Wells-next-the-Sea
A 149
B 1454
B 1105
B 1355
B 146
A 149
Blakeney
ingham House
akenham

The Wash

24

Sanquhar
732
Moffat
99
159
A 6088
29
Carter Bar
The Cheviot

OUT
Beattock
15
Annan
A 708
A 702
23
Thornhill
38
61
53
85
THE
NORTH
The Border
Forest
Park

8
AND
GALLOWAY
21
13
Lochmaben
17
Lockerbie
-9
Langholm
B 6357
24
A 709
13
18
Dumfries
A 74
Canonbie
A 7
A 711
14
A 710
22
29
47
Annan
16
73
A 75
22
Longtown
A 6071
11
Greenhead
A 69
S. Tyne
60
97
New Abbey
Gretna
7
6
A 7
Brampton
A 689
19
Dalbeattie
A 110
26
Bowness-on-Solway
5
73
A 69
44
43
Eden
Alston
A 686
Auchencairn
Firth
Siloth
23
Wigton
Carlisle
A 595
42
M6
A 6
A 686
A 6277
2

Solway
Abbey Town
A 596
B 5300
Thursby
20
Cross Fell
893
Maryport
28
55
34
A 595
Aspatria
Bothel
C U M B R I A
22
35
41
Penrith
20
Appleby
A 66
A 6
A 591
Cockermouth
Skiddaw
931
A 66
40
A 6260
21
Workington
8
A 66
15
Keswick
38
16
A 66
11
Orton
A 685
Kirk
Whitehaven
A 595
6
Frizington
Derwent water
61
Ullswater
12
M6
Tebay
A 685
St. Bees Head
Buttermere
B 5289
Rosthwaite
Patterdale
Shap
39
B 6260
A 684
Egremont
Lake District National Park
A 592
38
Orton
Gosforth
Scafell Pikes
977
949
Grasmere
Ambleside
32
A 6
A 685
57
92
Coniston
Bowness
Windermere
9
A 591
37
Sedbergh
A 683
Broughton-in-Furness
A 593
A5084
18
Kendal
A 684
43
A 595
Greenodd
A 590
A 5074
5
8
11
Whernside
736
A 65
Millom
Ulverston
12
17
B 5278
527
36
A 65
Kirkby Lonsdale
Dalton
A 590
19
Grange-Over-Sands
18
13
Ingleton
Clapham
Barrow-in-Furness
Carnforth
35 A
35
Lune
B 6480
40
64
Morecambe
D
Belfast
15
Heysham
Lancaster
560
11

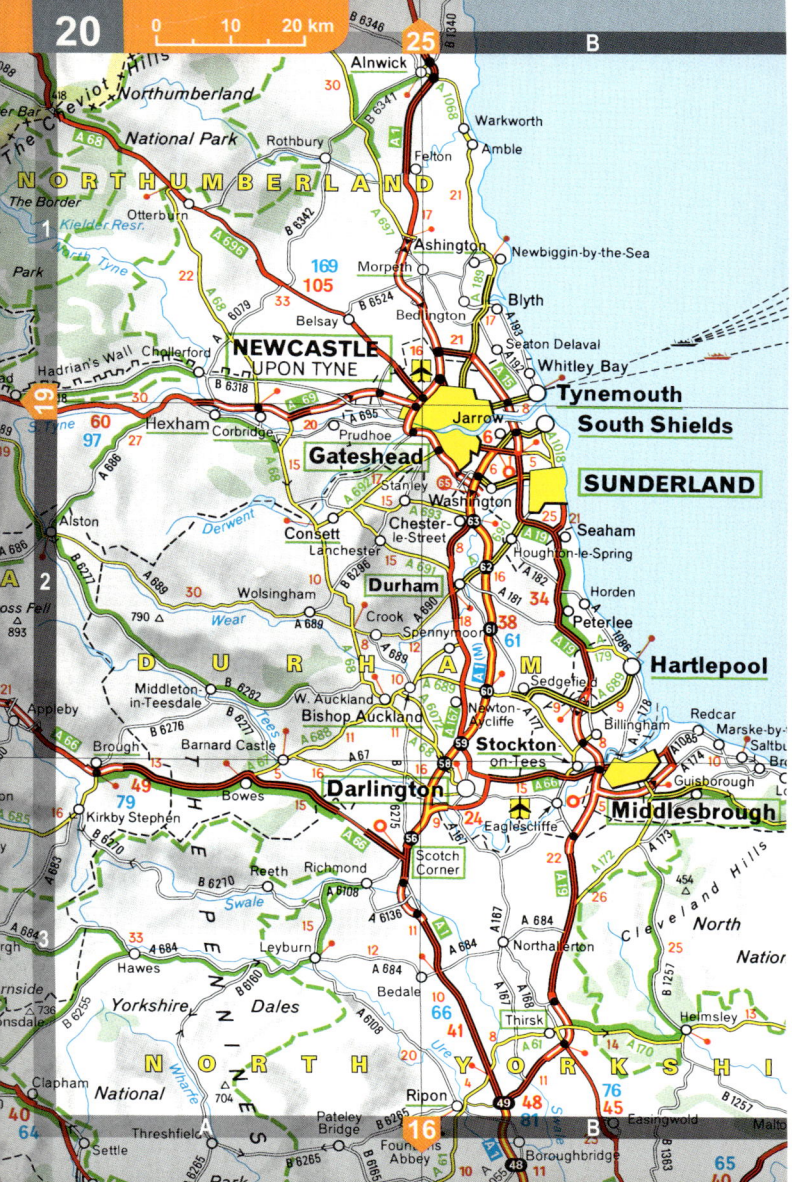

C

N O R T H   S E A

Bergen
Stavanger
Haugesund
Kristiansand
Göteborg

1

2

3

the-Sea
urn-by-the-Sea
otton
ottus
19
A 174
27
A 171
Whitby
21
A 169
21
York
Moors
A 171
al   Park
Scalby
Scarborough
Pickering
17
A 170
7
8
A 169
R   E   Filey
A 1039
22
A 64
Norton
C
17
Flamborough Head
B 1249
E R I D I N G
Bridlington

D

0   10   20 km

Scarinish

Tobermory

B 8073

Dervaig

27

B

19

A 848

10

Salen

Lochaline

Achnacro

L. Tuath

Ulva

A 849

Staffa

L. na Keal

MULL

11

Lismore

B 8035

△ 966

Craignure

Ben More

21

17

Kerrera

L. Scridain

18

A 849

Iona

Firth of Lorn

Fionnphort

Bunessan

A 844

Kiln

Seil

B

3

Luing

Arduain

Toberonochy

A 816

Scarba

△ 449

Colonsay

Crinan

Kiln

Scalasaig

B 841

Ardlussa

Lochgilphead

JURA

Ardrishaig

Rubha a' Mhail

Sound of Jura

Knapdale

2

784 △

19

Beinn an Oir

A 846

562 △

Port Askaig

Feolin

Tarbert

Ti

ISLAY

Ferry

A 846

25

Craighouse

Kenna

A 847

Bridgend

Port Charlotte

23

22

Claonaig

491 △

Portnahaven

Beinn Bheigeir

Kintyre

Gigha I.

Rinns Point

A 846

32

Ardbeg

Tayinloan

Mull of Oa

Port Ellen

41

Carradale

Kilbrannan Sound

A 842

3

A 83

Blackw

Machrihanish

Campbeltown

B 843

B 842

Antrim   Coast

Rathlin Island

Inishowen Head

Giant's Causeway

Mull of Kintyre

Portrush

26

Southend

Portstewart

A 29

astlerock

A 2

Fair H

47

B

Bushmills

Ballycastle

21

Coleraine

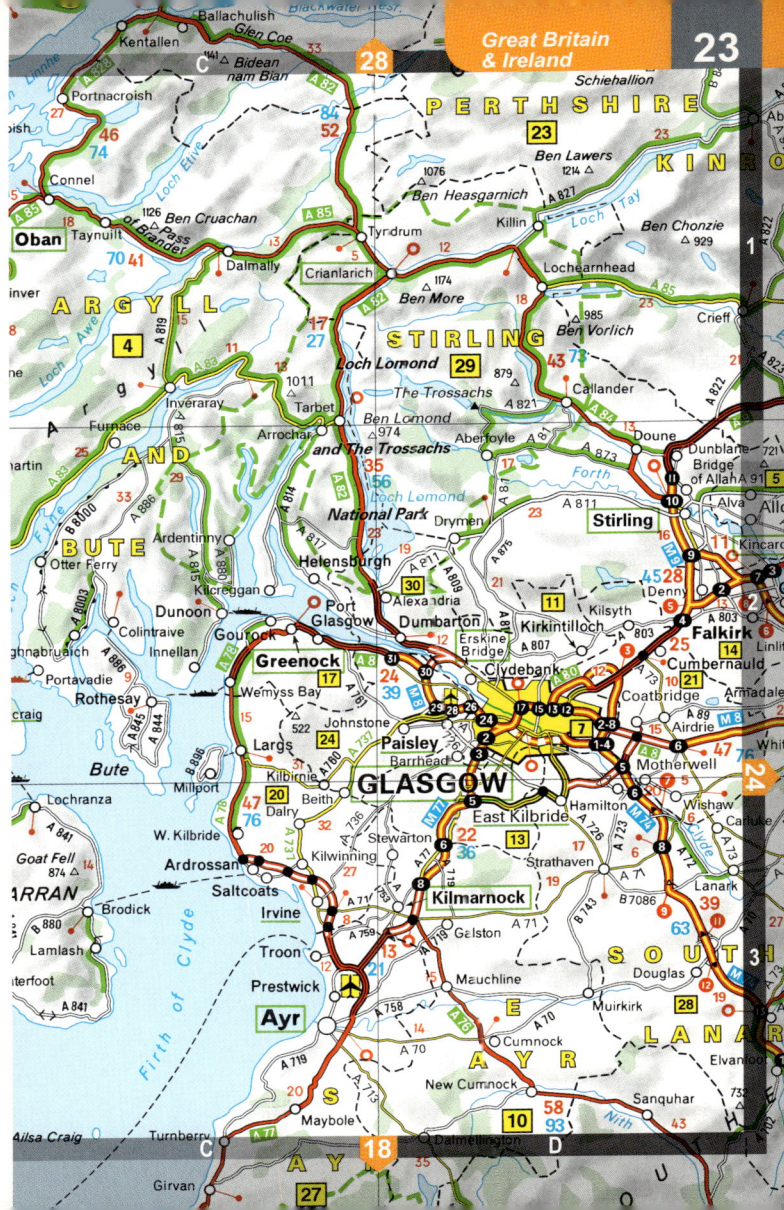

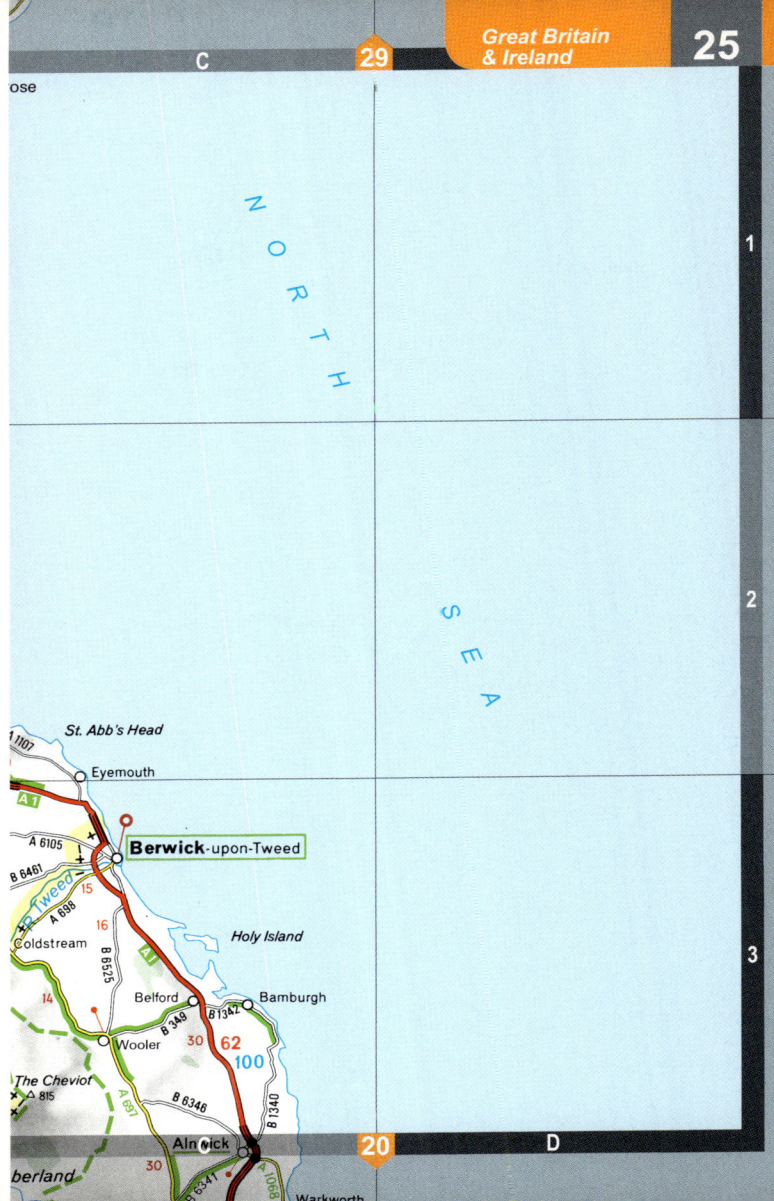

1

2

N O R T H

S E A

St. Abb's Head

Eyemouth

A 1

A 6105

Berwick-upon-Tweed

B 6461

Tweed

15

16

Coldstream

A 698

B 6525

14

Holy Island

Belford

B 349

B 1342

Bamburgh

Wooler

30

62

100

3

The Cheviot

△ 815

A 691

B 6346

B 1340

Alnwick

30

B 6341

1068

Warkworth

berland

ose

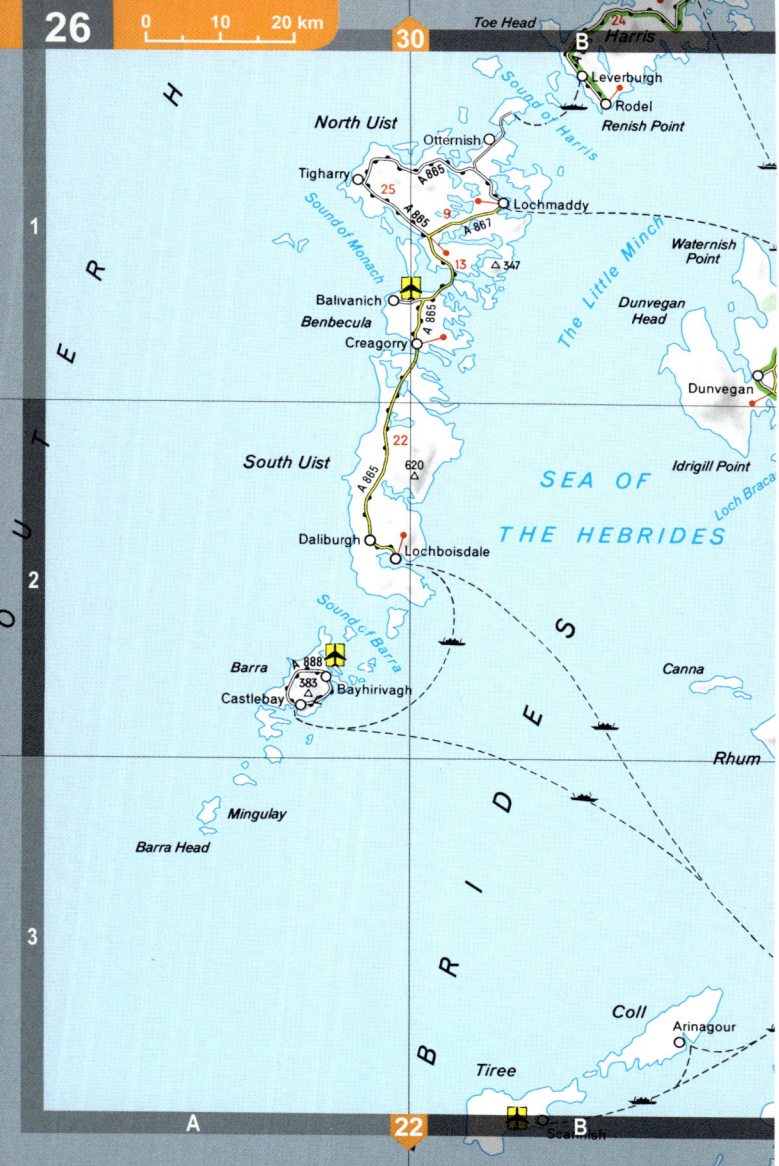

0   10   20 km

Toe Head

24

B   Harris

Leverburgh

Rodel

Renish Point

Sound of Harris

North Uist

Otternish

Tigharry

25

A 865

Lochmaddy

A 865

9

A 867

Waternish
Point

13

347

The Little Minch

Dunvegan
Head

Balivanich

Benbecula

A 865

Creagorry

Dunvegan

Sound of Monach

Sound of Monach

South Uist

22

A 865

620

SEA   OF

Idrigill Point

Loch Braca

THE   HEBRIDES

Daliburgh

Lochboisdale

Sound of Barra

O   U   T   E   R

H

Canna

Barra

888

Bayhirivagh

383

Castlebay

Mingulay

Barra Head

B   R   I   D   E   S

Rhum

Coll

Arinagour

Tiree

Scainish

1

2

3

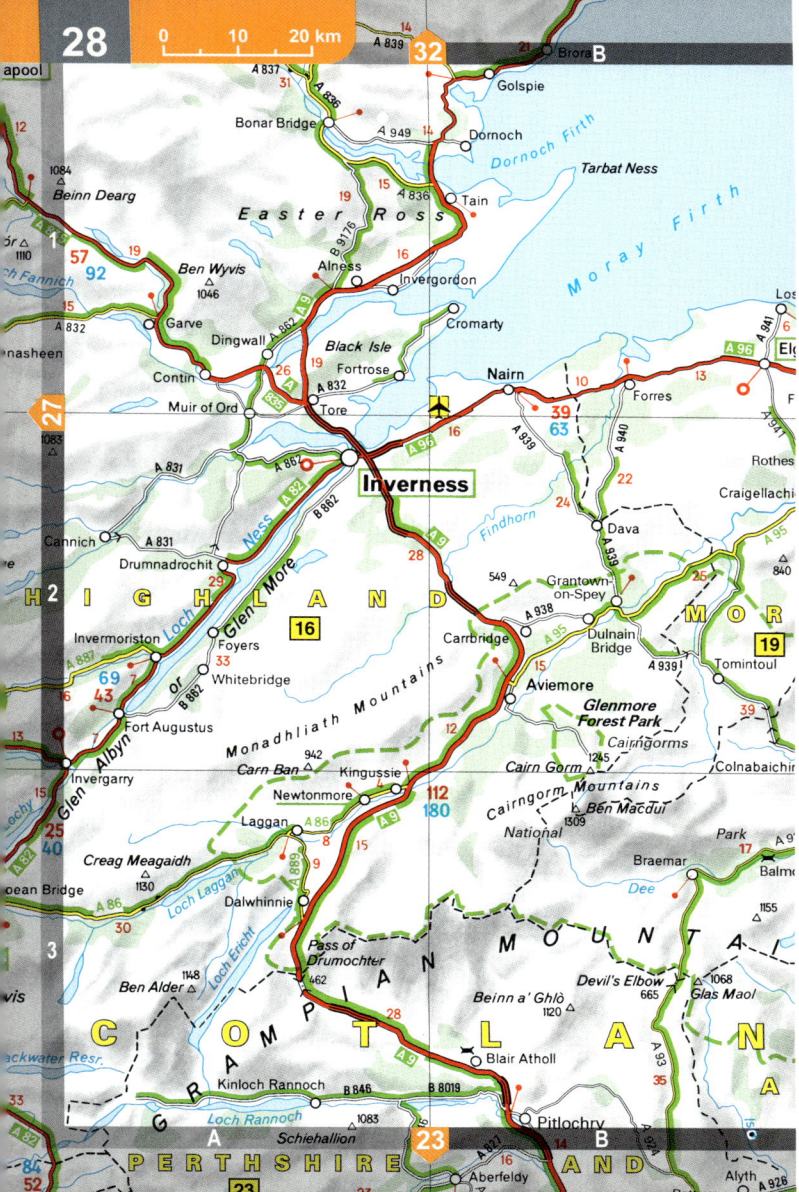

1

Great Britain & Ireland

ssiemouth

Buckie Cullen

gin

Banff Macduf

Kinnairds Head

Fraserburgh

ochabers

23

A 98

12

B 9031

26

A 98

A 90

Rattray Head

17

A 95

21

A 97

11

A 947

A 950

26

A 981

A 952

13

18

Keith

R. Spey

12

Deveron

B 9025

Turriff

New Deer

B 9029

Mintlaw

A 950 9

Peterhead

Dufftown

A 95

11

A 96

22

A 947

A 948

14

18

Buchan Ness

A 920

Huntly

A 97

18

B 9170

Ellon

A 975

Cruden Bay

2

15

66

109

A 920

23

Oldmeldrum

A 920

51

83

Newburgh

2

Rhynie

Mossat

A 944

Don

Inverurie

Kintore

18

A 947

15

A 944

Stromness

Lerwick

Torshavn

Alford

Craigievar
Castle

15

A 96

1

A 944

A 97

871

27

34

A 944

Aboyne

A 93

17

A 93

ABERDEEN

Crathes
Castle

Ballater

25

Banchory

Dee

18

A 957

oral Castle

14

N. Esk

Stonehaven

89

55

A 90

A 92

Laurencekirk

22

Inverbervie

3

D

Marikirk

22

GUS

S. Esk

A 926

Brechin

A 90

A 935

10

A 831

Kirriemuir

15

B 9113

A 934

A 92

Glamis
Castle

A 94

Forfar

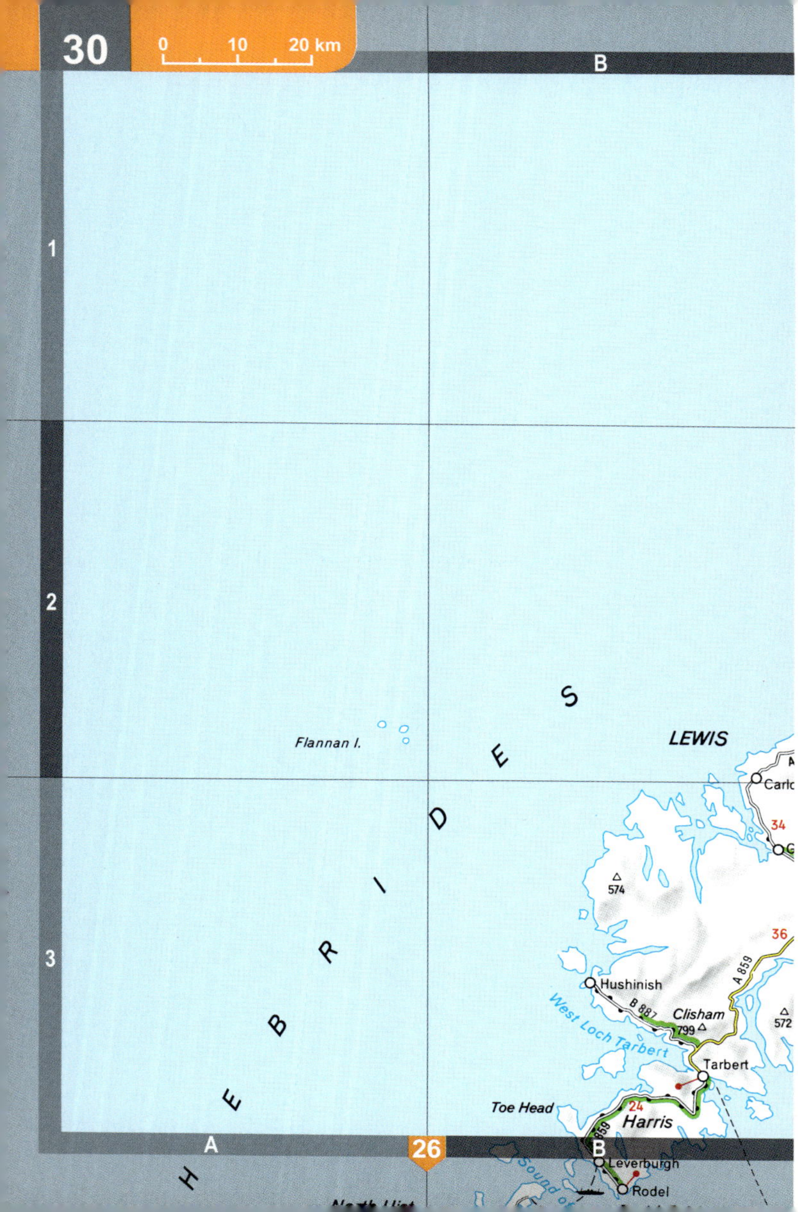

0   10   20 km

B

1

2

S

E

Flannan I.

LEWIS

D

Carl

34

C

I

574

Hushinish

36

B 887

Clisham

572

3

West Loch Tarbert

799

A 859

Tarbert

Toe Head

24

Harris

A

B

Leverburgh

H

Rodel

Sound of

North Uist

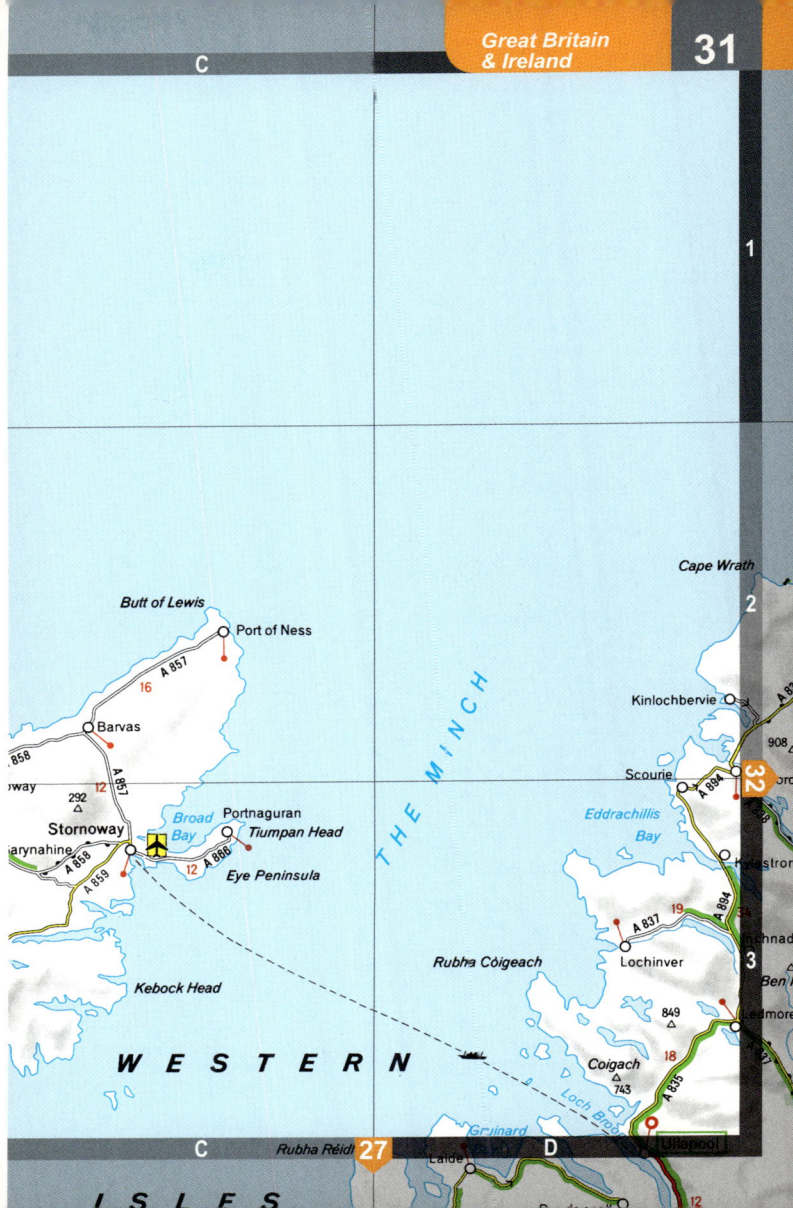

C

1

Cape Wrath

2

Butt of Lewis

Port of Ness

A 857

16

Kinlochbervie

A 83

Barvas

858

A 857

12

292

△

Stornoway

Broad Bay

Portnaguran

Tiumpan Head

arynahine

A 859

A 857

12

A 886

Eye Peninsula

A 859

908

△

Scourie

A 894

32

ord

Eddrachillis Bay

Kylestrom

T H E   M I N C H

A 894

83

A 837

19

Lochinver

ichnad

3

Ben M

Rubha Cóigeach

849

△

Ledmore

Kebock Head

W E S T E R N

Coigach

△

743

18

A 835

Loch Bro

Gruinard

Ullapool

Rubha Réidh

27

Laide

D

I S L E S

12

0   10   20 km

B

1

Lerwick

Main

Rora Head

Aberdeen

Cape Wrath

2

Durness   *Whiten Head*   *Strathy Point*   Scrabster

Kyle of Tongue

A 838   20   A 836   27 Melvich   16   A 836   **Thurso**

ervie   A 838   Loch Eriboll   A 838   31   Coldbackie   Bettyhill   Road

908 △ *Foinaven*   927   Tongue   △ 290   A 9

Laxford Bridge   *Ben Hope*   Syre   B 871   A 897

31   A 838   B 873   39   114   24

Kylestrome   Altnaharra   L. Naver   183

A 894   39   *Ben Klibreck*   B 871   Latheron

54   40   961 △   706 △ *Morven*

3   △ 998   713 △   *Ben Armine*   Kinbrace   20

Inchnadamph   *Ben More Assynt*   A 838   Loch Shin

Ledmore   A 897   Helmsdale

A 837   A 836   A 9

Lairg   14   A 839

pool   27 A 839   11   21   Brora

A 837   31   A 836   Golspie

12   Bonar Bridge   Firth

A   28   B

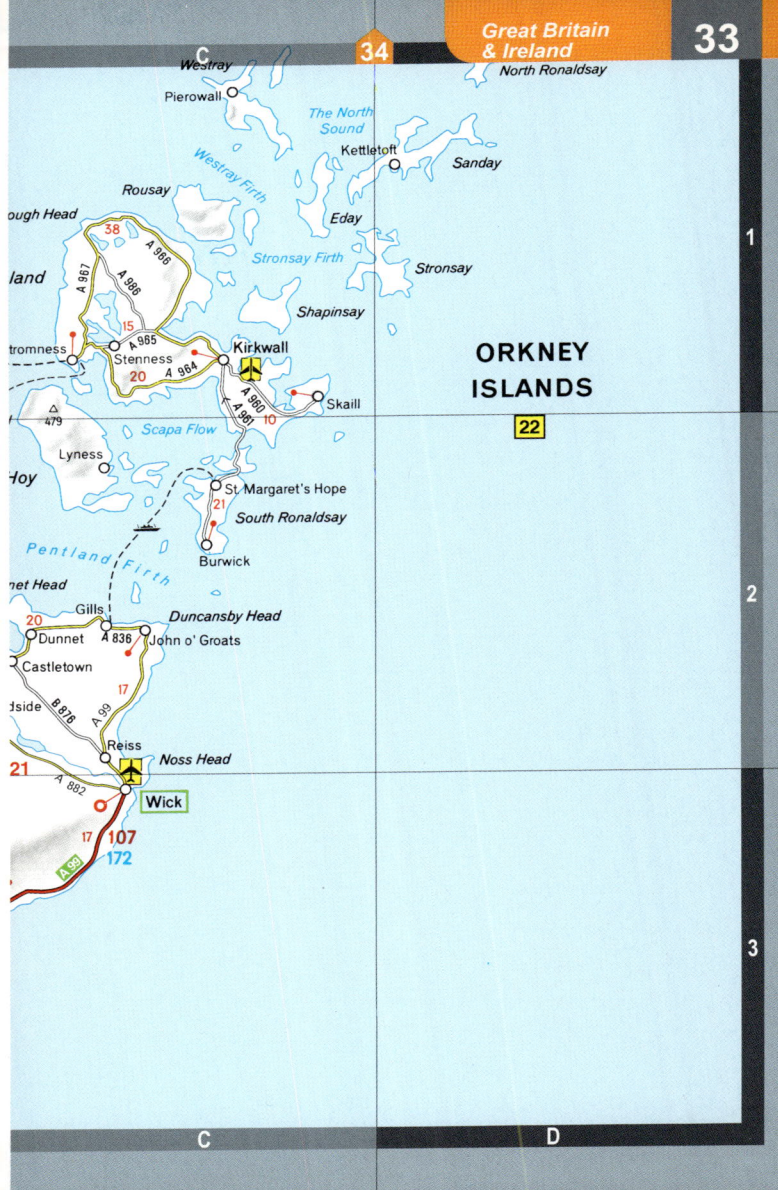

C

Westray

Pierowall

The North Sound

Kettletoft

Sanday

Westray Firth

Rousay

North Ronaldsay

ugh Head

38

A 967

A 966

A 966

Eday

Stronsay Firth

Stronsay

land

15

Shapinsay

tromness

A 965

Stenness

20

A 964

Kirkwall

A 960

A 961

10

Skaill

ORKNEY ISLANDS

22

479

Scapa Flow

Lyness

Hoy

St Margaret's Hope

21

South Ronaldsay

Burwick

Pentland Firth

net Head

20

Gills

Duncansby Head

Dunnet

A 836

John o' Groats

Castletown

17

dside

B 876

A 99

Reiss

Noss Head

21

A 882

Wick

17

107

A 99

172

1

2

3

C

D

0   10   20 km

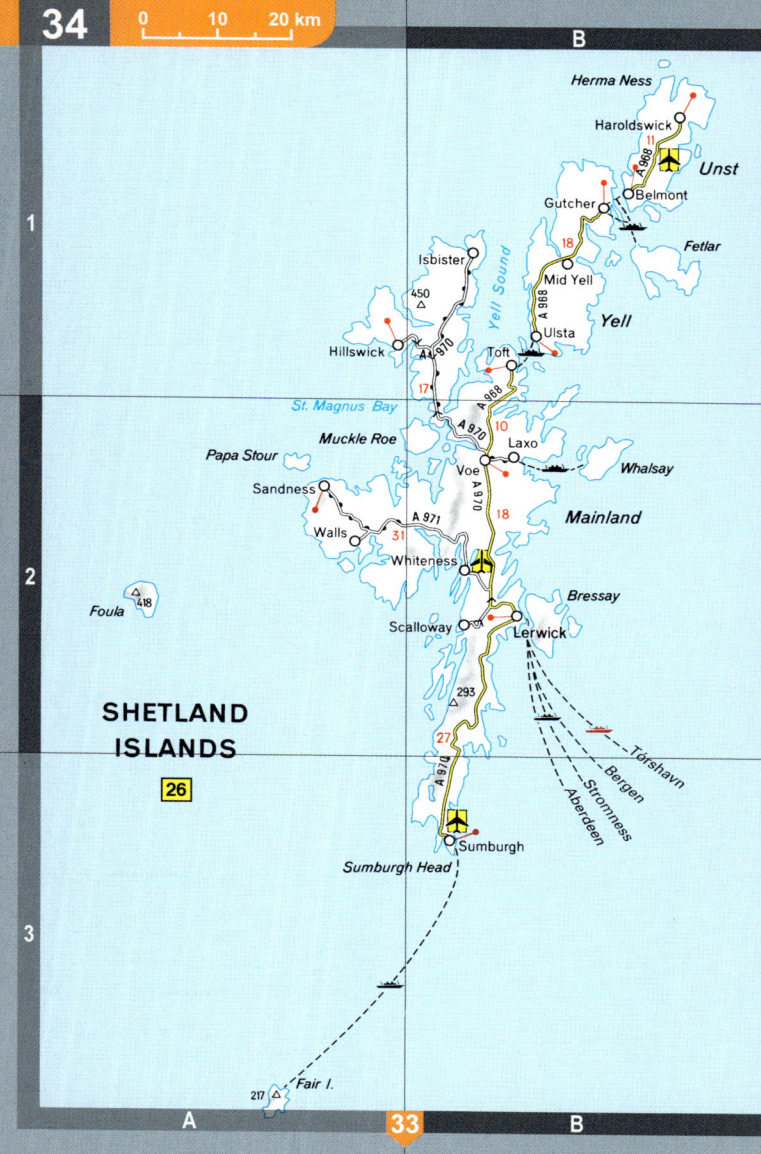

B

Herma Ness

Haroldswick

11

A 968

Unst

Belmont

Gutcher

18

Fetlar

1

Isbister

Yell Sound

Mid Yell

A 968

450 △

Yell

Hillswick

A 970

Ulsta

Toft

17

St. Magnus Bay

A 968

10

A 970

Laxo

Muckle Roe

Papa Stour

Voe

Whalsay

Sandness

A 971

18

Mainland

Walls

31

Whiteness

Bressay

2

Foula

418 △

Scalloway

Lerwick

293 △

Tórshavn

SHETLAND
ISLANDS

27

A 970

Bergen

Stromness

Aberdeen

26

Sumburgh

Sumburgh Head

3

217 △   *Fair I.*

A   B

C

Weymouth
Poole
Rosslare
Poole
Portsmouth

Cap de la Hague
Alderney
Nez de Jobourg

Cherbourg-Octeville
Cap L

Beaumont-Hague
29   D 901   SP   1
D 22   D 650   900   7
32   D 37

les Pieux
21   D 56   E 46   N 3 E 46   D 24
D 23   900   24
Valognes
D 23   900

Guernsey

Bricquebec
17   15   D 90   13

St. Peter Port
D 650
Barneville-Carteret
St Sauve le-V.
D 15

Sark
Carteret
D 903
D 900   55
19   11

Portbail
D 650   903

la Haye-du-Puits
28   8

Jersey
Gorey
Lessay
D 900
St-Hélier
D 650   **M A**
50

Portsmouth
Weymouth
St Malo-de-la-Lande
21   D 68
Agon-Coutainville
19   D 44   SP   C
4   D 2

Montmartin
30   15

I. Chausey
Bréhal
D 13   8
Gavr

Granville
D 971   D 13
26
D 924

St Pair
la Haye-Pesnel
Jullouville
D 61   3
Carolles   D 911   Sarti
32

St Quay-Portrieux
Cap Fréhel
St Malo
Paramé
Rothéneuf
Pte du Grouin
Avranches

Sables-d'Or
Dinard
St Lunaire
Cancale
le Mont-St Michel

Binic
Erquy
St Cast
St Briac
D 355
le Vivier
22   D 43
15
le Val-André
D 34
St Jacut
SP
St Servan
155   E 401   N 176   797   N 175
Pléneuf
Matignon
D 786   D 168
Châteauneuf
16
31
Pontorson
St Brieuc
D 17   794   Ploubalay
23
12   E 401   N 176   D 19   Pontorson
Fougères

Plancoët
47
176   Dol-de-Ble   Fougères
Lamballe
Dinan

0   10   20 km

R 487

Kilrush   Killim

Loop Head

Kilbaha

Mouth of
the Shannon

Ballybunnion   11

R 551

Ballyduff   R 553   Listowel

Kerry Head   R 551   R 556   17   Feale   R 555   10   Abbeyfeale

Ballyheige   R 556   N 69   14

Brandon Head   Tralee Bay   Tralee   Trá Lí   N 21   65   12   Castleisland   R 577

Sybil Head   △951   Brandon Mountain   N 86   850   90   N 22   109

Clogher Head   Dingle   △825   Slieve Mish Mts.   34   20   15   68

Great Blasket I.   516   △   Dingle   Anascaul   31   N 86   N 70   R 561

Slea Head   N 86   Castlemaine   R 561

Dingle Bay   Killorglin   16   K E R R Y

Glenbeigh   L. Caragh   86   N 72   Killarney / Cill Airne

Doulus Head   689 △   N 70   25   Muckross House   L. Leane   N 72   Rath

Knight's Town   772   Carrantuohill   △838   694

Valencia Island   Cahersiveen   1038   Macgillycuddy's Reeks   N 22

St. Finan's Bay   10   Iveragh   Mangerton Mountain   17   Derrynas   87

Waterville   L. Currane   Ring   of Kerry   21   Kilgarvan   R 569   54

Bolus Head   22   Sneem   17   Kenmare

Skellig   30

Kenmare River   Lauragh   17   30

Beara   △706   Pass of Ke

Castletownbere   R 571   Caha Mts.   Glengarriff   Dunma

Dursey Island   L 61   △684   21   R 572   3   Bantry / Beanntraí   R 586

Bere I.   Bantry Bay   19   R 593

Sheep's Head   R 591   10

Dunmanus Bay   Skull   N 71   Skibbereen

Mizen Head   18   R 591   R 592   10

Roaringwater Bay   Toe Head

Clear Island

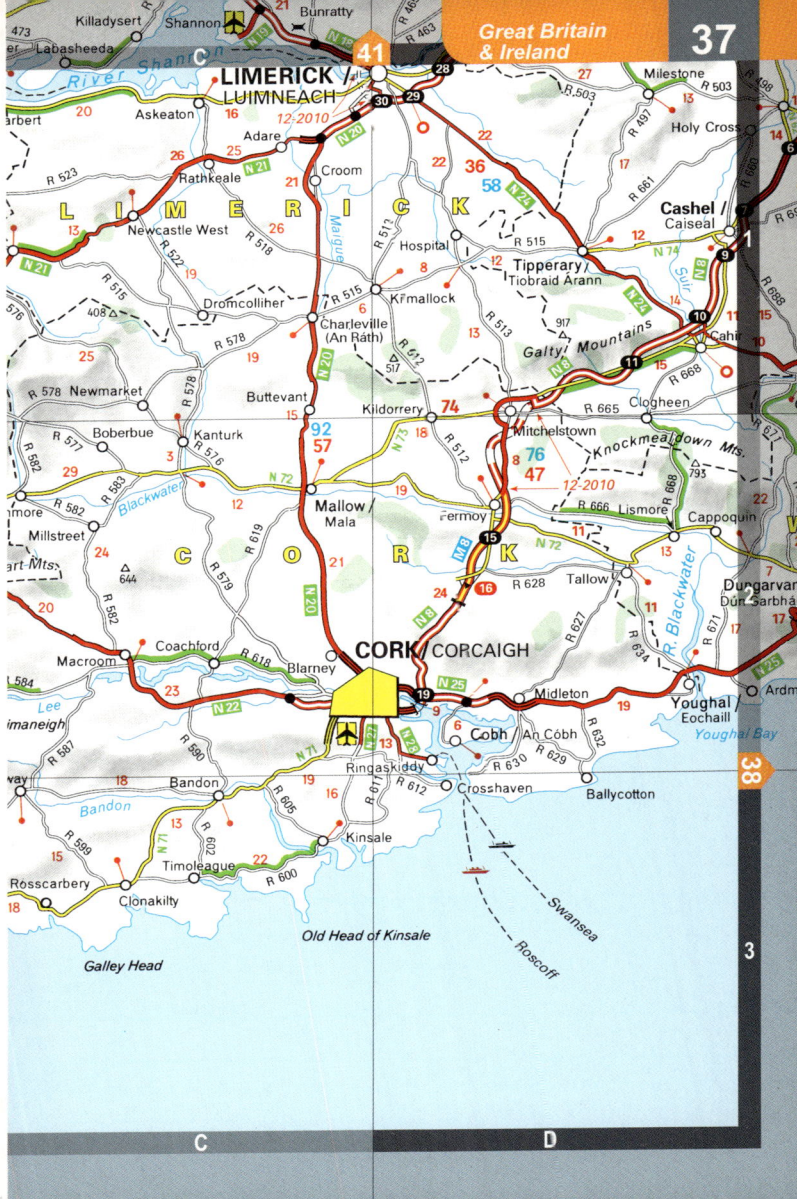

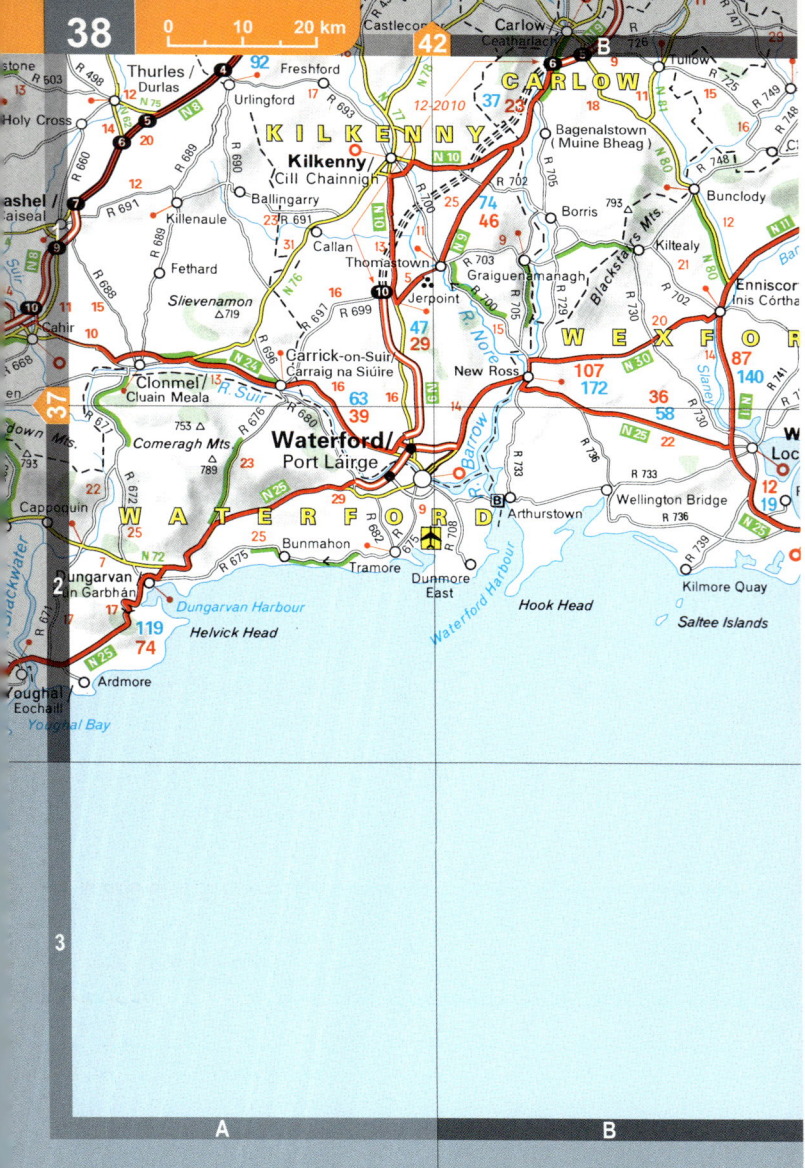

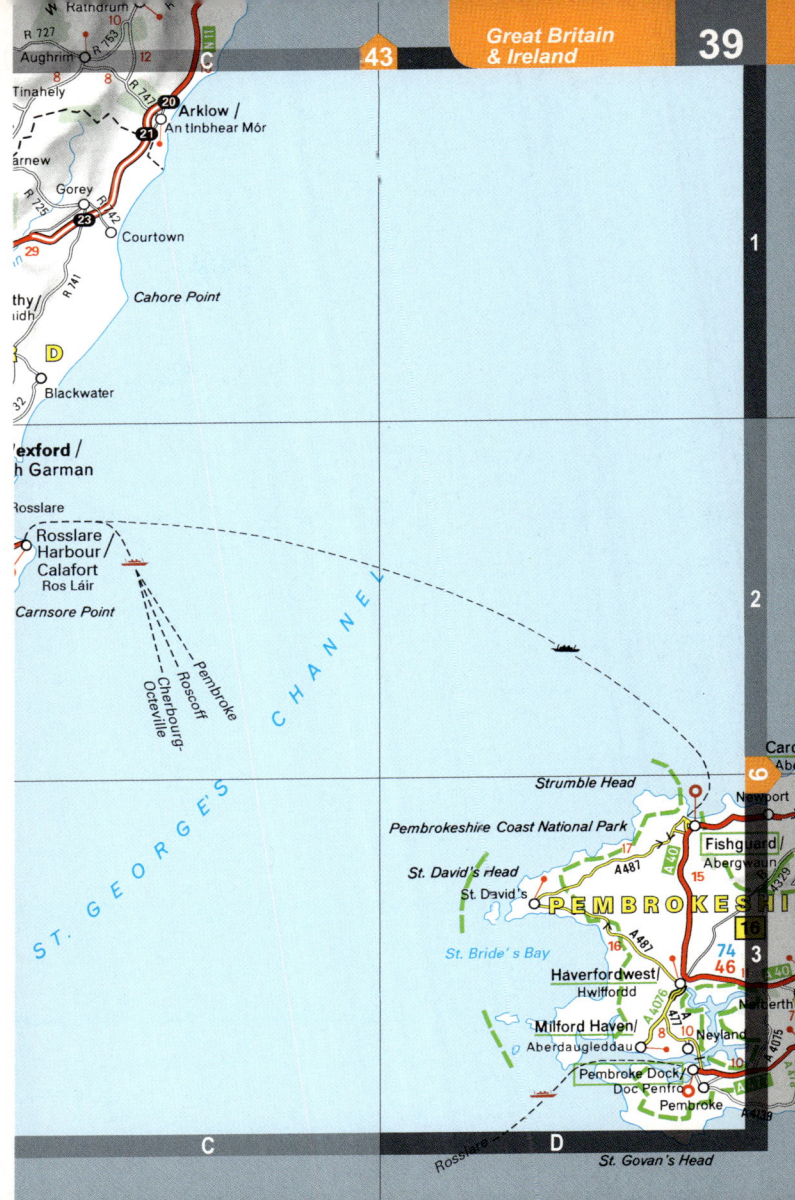

1

2

3

Rathdrum

R 727

Aughrim

Tinahely

20 Arklow /
An tInbhear Mór

21

arnew

Gorey

23

R 742

Courtown

R 741

29

Cahore Point

thy
 idh

D

Blackwater

exford /
h Garman

Rosslare

Rosslare
Harbour /
Calafort
Ros Láir

Carnsore Point

Pembroke
Roscoff
Cherbourg-
Octeville

S T. G E O R G E ' S   C H A N N E L

Strumble Head

Pembrokeshire Coast National Park

St. David's Head

St. David's

PEMBROKESHI

St. Bride's Bay

A487

Newport

Card
Abe

6

Fishguard /
Abergwaun

A40

15

1 6

74
46

3

Haverfordwest
Hwlffordd

A4076

Nolberth

Milford Haven /
Aberdaugleddau

8

10

Neyland

Pembroke Dock /
Doc Penfro

10

Pembroke

A4139

C

D

Rosslare

St. Govan's Head

0   10   20 km

Achill Island 17
R 313
Corraun   Mulra
Clare Island   Clew Bay
Louisburgh R 335 **14**
△ Croagh P
Inishturk   **20**
Murrisk
Inishbofin   Mweelrea Mts.
Inishshark   △ 817
Rinvyle Pt.   R 335
Killary Harbour
Letterfrack   **22** Leenane
The Twelve Pins   R 59   **9**
△ 728 701△ Maumturk Mts.
Connemara
Clifden **22**
An Clochán   N 59
Slyne Head R 341
Roundstone   Maam Cross
Gortmore
Carna R 340
12
Kilkieran Bay
Lettermullan R 374
Gorumna Island

A r a n

Inishmore
Kilronan
Inishi
I s l a n d s
Inisheer

Cliffs of Moher
La

Spanish Point
29

N 67
Kilkee N 67 R 483
8
R 487
Kilrush **6** Killin
△ R

Loop Head Kilbaha
Mouth of R 551
the Shannon Ballybunnion **11** T

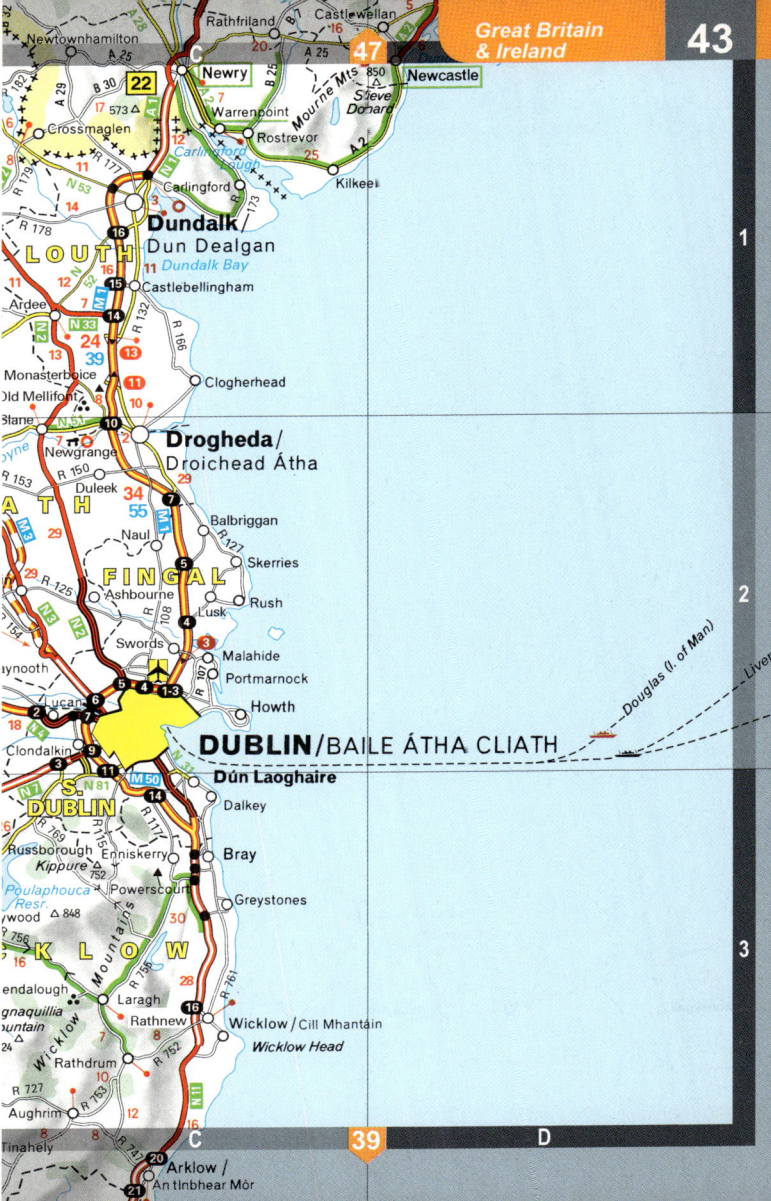

Rathfriland
Castlewellan
Newtownhamilton
Newry
Newcastle
Slieve Donard 850
Warrenpoint
Rostrevor
Crossmaglen
Carlingford Lough
Kilkeel
Carlingford

Dundalk/
Dun Dealgan
Dundalk Bay

L O U T H
Castlebellingham
Ardee
Monasterboice
Old Mellifont
Clogherhead

Newgrange
Drogheda/
Droichead Átha

Duleek
Balbriggan

M E A T H
Naul
Skerries

F I N G A L
Ashbourne
Rush
Lusk
Swords

Maynooth
Malahide
Portmarnock
Lucan
Howth

Clondalkin

DUBLIN/BAILE ÁTHA CLIATH

S. **DUBLIN**
Dún Laoghaire

Dalkey
Russborough
Enniskerry
Kippure
Bray
Powerscourt

Poulaphouca Resr
Greystones

K L O W

Glendalough
Lugnaquillia Mountain
Laragh
Rathnew
Wicklow/Cill Mhantain
Rathdrum
Wicklow Head

Aughrim

Tinahely

Arklow/
An tInbhear Mór

Douglas (I. of Man)
Liverpool

0   10   20 km

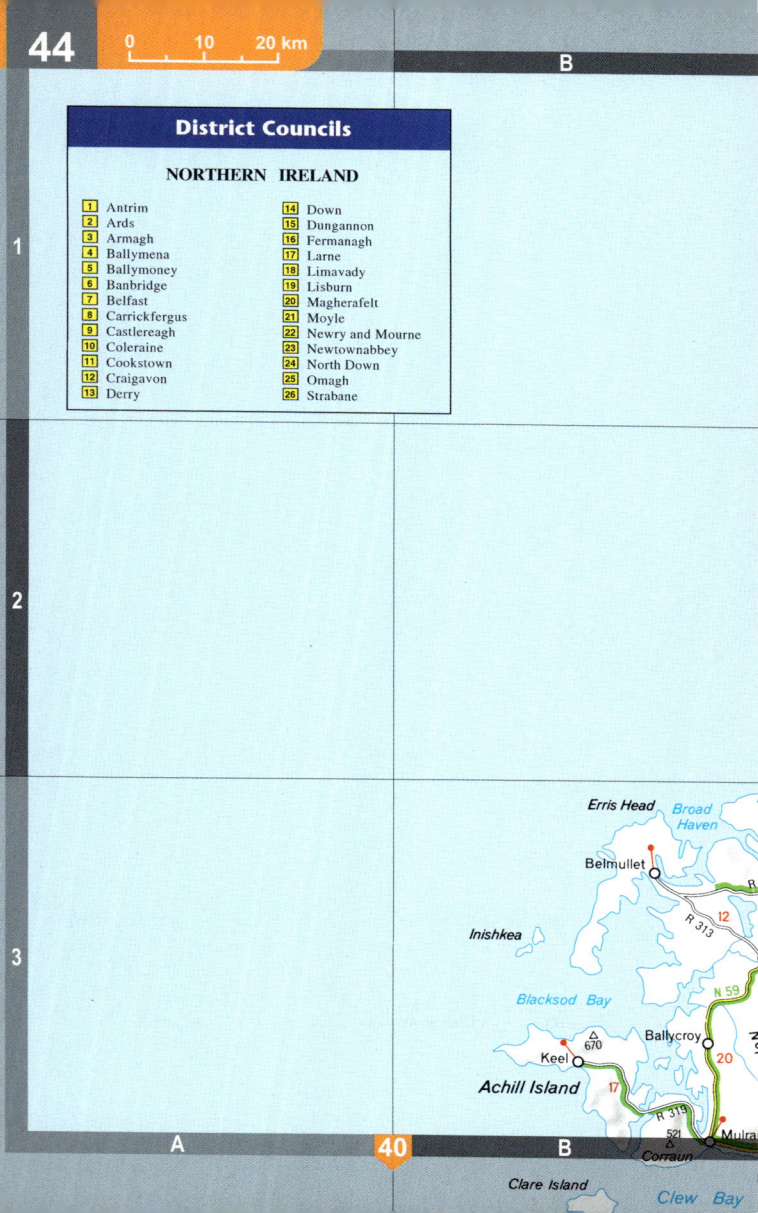

District Councils

NORTHERN IRELAND

1	Antrim	14	Down
2	Ards	15	Dungannon
3	Armagh	16	Fermanagh
4	Ballymena	17	Larne
5	Ballymoney	18	Limavady
6	Banbridge	19	Lisburn
7	Belfast	20	Magherafelt
8	Carrickfergus	21	Moyle
9	Castlereagh	22	Newry and Mourne
10	Coleraine	23	Newtownabbey
11	Cookstown	24	North Down
12	Craigavon	25	Omagh
13	Derry	26	Strabane

Erris Head

Broad Haven

Belmullet

R 313

12

Inishkea

N 59

Blacksod Bay

Ballycroy

20

670

Keel

Achill Island

17

R 319

521

Mulra

Corraun

Clare Island

Clew Bay

1

2

3

A

40

B

C

Bloody Forela
Head

1

Aran Island

Gweebarra Bay

N 56

R 261

Rossan Point

Glencolumbkille

Ardara

R 263

20

N 56

15

2

Killybegs

15

D o n e g a l   B a y

Bundoran/
Bun Dobhrá

46

Inishmurray

65

40

L. Melvin

23

N15

644

16

31

Ballycastle

Easky

Rosses Point

314

Glenamoy

379

R 314

Killala
Bay

R 297

Sligo Bay

Strandhill

Sligo

Sligeach

15

4

L. Gill

3

Bangor

M A Y O

R 315

12

17

Inishcrone

33

N 59

R 282

Ballysadare

R 287

Drumkeeran

R 280

20

N 59

L. Conn

7

Ballina /
Béal an Átha

T h e   O x   M o u n t a i n s

543

N 59

S L I G O

R 284

19

Crossmolina

R 312

10

R 294

29

M17

Keadew

698

804

N 5

R 310

20

47

Ballymote

21

R 293

20

L. Arrow

720

Nephin

R 315

25

Foxford

Tobercurry

18

7

L. Key

Range

Pontoon

25

Castlebar /
Caisleán an
Bharraigh

C

41

39

Charlestown

Gorteen

Boyle /
Mainistir
na Búille

Newport

N 5

8

24

L. Gara

11

0   10   20 km

B

Inishtrahull

Malin Head

Tory I.

Fanad Head

Bloody Foreland Head

Dunfanaghy

Creeslough

Errigal Mt. △752

Carrigart

Portsalon

Inishowen
△615
Slieve Snaght

Culdaff

Carndonagh

R 238

R 241

Moville

Lough Foyle

A 2

Crolly

Dunglow

Derryveagh Mountains

Millford

Rathmullan

Rathmelton

Buncrana

Quigley's Point

Muff

R 245

R 246

R 247

R 255

Letterkenny / Leitir Ceanainn

Grianán of Aileach

Eglinton

Limavady

Londonderry / Derry

Fintown

R 252

R 250

R 236

R 237

Claudy

Dunnamanagh

Glenties

Stranorlar

Ballybofey

Lifford

Strabane

Plumbridge

Sperrin Mountains
Sawel Mountain
△680

Ardara

Blue Stack Mts.
672△

Finn

Castlederg

Newtownstewart

Mourne

Gortin

Donegal / Dún na nGall

Lough Derg

Pettigoe

Kesh

Dromore

Omagh

A 505

Cookstown

NORTHERN

Ballyshannon

R 232

R 233

A 35

B 4

Ballintra / Baile an Dobhráin

Belleek

Irvinestown

Lower Lough Erne

Fintona

Dungannon

12-2010

Ballygawley

Aughnacloy

IRELAND

Manorhamilton

L. Melvin
△644

Belcoo

Enniskillen

Fivemiletown

Armagh

R 200

R 281

Dowra
△667

Swanlinbar

Lisnaskea

Rossiea

Monaghan / Muineachán

Upper Lough Erne

Newtownbutler

Clones

Keady

Drumkeeran

Lough Allen

Ballyconnell

Belturbet

MONAGHAN

Arrow

Keadew

Drumshanbo

Ballinamore

LEITRIM

Carrick-on-Shannon

Killashandra

Cootehill

Place name index

Place name ⟶ Cambridge .... 12 B 2 ⟵ Grid reference in the atlas

Refers to the page

A

Abbey Town .... **19** **C 2**
Abbots Bromley .... **16** **A 3**
Abbotsbury ....**4** **B 2**
Aberaeron ....**9** **D 2**
Aberdare / Aberdâr .... **10** **A 3**
Aberdaron .... **14** **A 3**
Aberdeen .... **29** **D 3**
Aberdovey / Aberdyfi ....**9** **D 1**
Aberfeldy .... **24** **A 1**
Aberfoyle .... **23** **D 2**
Abergavenny / Y-Fenni .... **10** **A 3**
Abergele .... **14** **B 2**
Aberlady .... **24** **B 2**
Abermaw / Barmouth .... **14** **B 3**
Aberporth ....**9** **C 2**
Abersoch .... **14** **A 3**
Abertillery .... **10** **A 3**
Aberystwyth ....**9** **D 1**
Abingdon .... **11** **D 3**
Abington
  (South Lanarkshire) .... **24** **A 3**
Aboyne .... **29** **C 3**
Accrington .... **15** **D 1**
Achnacroish .... **22** **B 1**
Achnasheen .... **27** **D 1**
Acle .... **13** **D 1**
Ainsdale .... **15** **C 2**
Airdrie .... **23** **D 2**
Alcester .... **11** **C 2**
Aldeburgh .... **13** **D 3**
Aldershot ....**6** **A 1**
Alexandria .... **23** **D 2**
Alford (Aberdeenshire) ...... **29** **C 2**
Alford (Lincs.) .... **17** **C 3**
Alfreton .... **16** **A 3**
Alloa .... **24** **A 2**
Alness .... **28** **A 1**
Alnwick .... **20** **A 1**
Alston .... **19** **D 2**
Altnaharra .... **32** **A 3**
Alton (Hants.)......................**5** **D 1**
Altrincham .... **15** **D 2**
Alva .... **24** **A 2**
Alyth .... **24** **A 1**
Amble .... **20** **B 1**

Ambleside .... **19** **D 3**
Amersham ....**6** **A 1**
Amesbury ....**5** **C 1**
Amlwch .... **14** **A 2**
Ammanford / Rhydaman ......**9** **D 3**
Ampthill .... **12** **A 3**
Andover ....**5** **D 1**
Annan .... **19** **C 1**
Anstruther .... **24** **B 2**
Antrim .... **47** **C 2**
Appleby .... **19** **D 3**
Arbroath .... **24** **B 1**
Ardberg .... **22** **B 3**
Ardentinny .... **23** **C 2**
Ardglass .... **47** **D 3**
Ardlussa .... **22** **B 2**
Ardrishaig .... **22** **B 2**
Ardrossan .... **23** **C 3**
Arduaine .... **22** **B 1**
Ardvasar .... **27** **C 2**
Arinagour .... **26** **B 3**
Arisaig .... **27** **C 3**
Armadale (West Lothian) ...... **24** **A 2**
Armagh .... **47** **C 3**
Arrochar .... **23** **C 2**
Arundel ....**6** **A 2**
Ashbourne .... **16** **A 3**
Ashburton ....**3** **D 2**
Ashby de la Zouch .... **11** **C 1**
Ashford (Kent) ....**7** **C 2**
Ashington (Northumb.) ...... **20** **B 1**
Ashton-under-Lyne .... **15** **D 2**
Aspatria .... **19** **C 2**
Atherstone .... **11** **C 1**
Attleborough .... **13** **C 2**
Auchencairn .... **19** **C 2**
Auchterarder .... **24** **A 1**
Auchtermuchty .... **24** **A 1**
Audlem .... **15** **D 3**
Aughnacloy .... **46** **B 3**
Avebury ....**5** **C 1**
Aviemore .... **28** **B 2**
Avonmouth .... **10** **B 3**
Axminster ....**4** **A 2**
Aylesbury .... **11** **D 2**
Aylsham .... **13** **C 1**
Ayr .... **23** **C 3**

B

Bakewell .... **16** **A 3**
Bala .... **14** **B 3**
Baldock .... **12** **A 3**
Balivanich .... **26** **A 1**
Ballachulish .... **27** **D 3**
Ballantrae .... **18** **A 1**
Ballater .... **29** **C 3**
Ballaugh .... **18** **B 3**
Ballycastle (Antrim) .... **47** **C 1**
Ballyclare (Antrim) .... **47** **D 2**
Ballygawley (Dungannon).... **46** **B 3**
Ballymena .... **47** **C 2**
Ballymoney (Antrim) .... **47** **C 1**
Ballynahinch .... **47** **D 3**
Bamburgh Castle .... **25** **C 3**
Bampton (Devon) ....**4** **A 1**
Banbridge .... **47** **C 3**
Banbury .... **11** **D 2**
Banchory .... **29** **C 3**
Banff .... **29** **C 1**
Bangor (Gwynedd) .... **14** **B 2**
Bangor (North-Down) .... **47** **D 2**
Bargoed .... **10** **A 3**
Barlby .... **16** **B 1**
Barmouth / Abermaw .... **14** **B 3**
Barnard Castle .... **20** **A 3**
Barnsley .... **16** **A 2**
Barnstaple ....**3** **D 1**
Barrhead .... **23** **D 2**
Barrhill .... **18** **B 1**
Barrow-in-Furness .... **19** **C 3**
Barry / Barri
  (Vale of Glamorgan)..............**4** **A 1**
Barton-upon-Humber .... **17** **C 2**
Barvas .... **31** **C 2**
Basildon (Essex)..................**6** **B 1**
Basingstoke ....**5** **D 1**
Baslow .... **16** **A 3**
Bath ....**4** **B 1**
Bathgate .... **24** **A 2**
Battle ....**6** **B 2**
Bawtry .... **16** **B 2**
Bayhirivagh .... **26** **A 2**
Beaconsfield ....**6** **A 1**
Beaminster ....**4** **B 2**

Beattock	19	C 1
Beaulieu	5	D 2
Beaumaris	14	B 2
Bebington	15	C 2
Beccles	13	D 2
Beckington	5	C 1
Bedale	20	A 3
Beddgelert	14	B 3
Bedford	12	A 3
Bedlington	20	B 1
Bedwas	10	A 3
Bedworth	11	C 1
Beeford	17	C 1
Beith	23	C 3
Belcoo	46	A 3
Belfast	47	D 3
Belford	25	C 3
Belleek *(Fermanagh)*	46	A 3
Belper	16	A 3
Belsay	20	A 1
Benfleet	7	C 1
Bentley	16	B 2
Bere Regis	5	C 2
Berkhamsted	12	A 3
Berwick-upon-Tweed	25	C 3
Bethesda	14	B 2
Bettyhill	32	B 2
Betws-y-Coed	14	B 3
Beverley	17	C 1
Bewdley	10	B 1
Bexhill	6	B 2
Bibury	11	C 3
Bicester	11	D 3
Biddenden	7	C 2
Bideford	3	D 1
Biggar	24	A 3
Biggleswade	12	A 3
Billericay	6	B 1
Billingham	20	B 2
Billingshurst	6	A 2
Bingham	16	B 3
Bingley	16	A 1
Birchington	7	D 1
Birkenhead	15	C 2
Birmingham	11	C 1
Bishop Auckland	20	A 2
Bishop's Castle	10	A 1
Bishop's Stortford	12	B 3
Blackburn *(Lancs.)*	15	D 1
Blackpool	15	C 1
Blackwaterfoot	23	C 3
Blaenau Ffestiniog	14	B 3
Blaenavon	10	A 3
Blair Atholl	28	B 3
Blairgowrie	24	A 1
Blakeney *(Norfolk)*	13	C 1

Blandford Forum	5	C 2
Bletchley	11	D 2
Blyth *(Northumb.)*	20	B 1
Bo' Ness	24	A 2
Bodmin	3	C 2
Bognor Regis	6	A 3
Bolton	15	D 2
Bonar Bridge	28	A 1
Bootle *(Merseyside)*	15	C 2
Boroughbridge	16	A 1
Boston	12	A 1
Bothel	19	C 2
Botley	5	D 2
Bourne	12	A 1
Bournemouth	5	C 2
Bovey Tracey	4	A 2
Bowes	20	A 3
Bowness-on-Solway	19	D 2
Bowness-on-Windermere	19	D 3
Bracadale	27	C 2
Brackley	11	D 2
Bracknell	6	A 1
Bradford	16	A 1
Bradford-on-Avon	5	C 1
Brading	5	D 2
Bradwell-on-Sea	13	C 1
Braemar	28	B 3
Braintree	12	B 3
Brampton *(Cumbria)*	19	D 2
Brandon *(Suffolk)*	12	B 2
Braunton	3	D 1
Brechin	29	C 3
Brecon / Aberhonddu	10	A 2
Brentwood	6	B 1
Bridge of Allan	23	D 2
Bridgend *(Islay)*	22	A 2
Bridgend / Pen-y-bont (Bridgend)	9	D 3
Bridgnorth	10	B 1
Bridgwater	4	B 1
Bridlington	17	C 1
Bridport	4	B 2
Brigg	17	C 2
Brighouse	16	A 1
Brightlingsea	13	C 3
Brighton	6	B 2
Bristol	4	B 1
Brixham	4	A 3
Broadford	27	C 2
Broadstairs	7	D 1
Broadway	11	C 2
Brodick	23	C 3
Bromsgrove	11	C 2
Bromyard	10	B 2
Brora	32	B 3
Brotton	20	B 3

Brough	20	A 3
Broughshane	47	C 2
Broughton-in-Furness	19	C 3
Brownhills	11	C 1
Bruton	4	B 1
Brynmawr	10	A 3
Buckfastleigh	3	D 3
Buckhaven	24	B 2
Buckie	29	C 1
Buckingham	11	D 2
Bude	3	C 2
Budleigh Salterton	4	A 2
Builth Wells / Llanfair-ym-Muallt	10	A 2
Bunessan	22	B 1
Bungay	13	C 2
Buntingford	12	A 3
Burford	11	C 3
Burgess Hill	6	B 2
Burnham-on-Crouch	7	C 1
Burnham-on-Sea	4	B 1
Burnley	15	D 1
Burntisland	24	A 2
Burry Port / Porth Tywyn	9	C 3
Burton-upon-Trent	11	C 1
Bury	15	D 2
Bury St Edmunds	12	B 2
Bushmills	47	C 1
Buttermere	19	C 2
Buxton *(Derbs.)*	16	A 1

C

Caernarfon	14	A 2
Caerphilly / Caerffili	10	A 3
Caersws	10	A 1
Cairnryan	18	A 1
Caistor	17	C 2
Callander	23	D 1
Callington	3	D 2
Calne	5	C 1
Camberley	6	A 1
Camborne	2	B 3
Cambridge	12	B 2
Camelford	3	C 2
Campbeltown	22	B 3
Cannich	28	A 2
Cannock	11	C 1
Canonbie	19	D 1
Canterbury	7	C 1
Canvey Island	7	C 1
Capel Curig	14	B 3
Cardiff / Caerdydd	10	A 3
Cardigan / Aberteifi	9	C 2
Carlisle	19	D 2
Carloway	30	B 2
Carluke	23	D 3

Carmarthen / Caerfyrddin ......**9** C 2
Carnforth ....**19** D 3
Carnlough ....**47** D 2
Carnoustie ....**24** B 1
Carnwath ....**24** A 3
Carradale ....**22** B 3
Carrbridge ....**28** B 2
Carrickfergus ....**47** D 2
Castle Douglas ....**19** C 1
Castlebay ....**26** A 2
Castledawson ....**47** C 2
Castlederg ....**46** A 2
Castleford ....**16** A 1
Castlerock ....**47** C 1
Castleton (Derbs.) ....**16** A 2
Castletown ....**33** C 2
Castletown (Isle of Man)......**18** A 3
Castlewellan ....**47** D 3
Cerrigydrudion ....**14** B 3
Chapel-en-le-Frith ....**16** A 2
Chard ....**4** B 2
Chatham ....**7** C 1
Chatteris ....**12** A 2
Chelmsford ....**12** B 3
Cheltenham ....**10** B 3
Chepstow / Cas-Gwent ......**10** B 3
Cheshunt ....**6** B 1
Chester ....**15** C 3
Chester-le-Street ....**20** B 2
Chesterfield ....**16** A 3
Chichester ....**6** A 2
Chippenham ....**5** C 1
Chipping Campden ....**11** C 2
Chipping Norton ....**11** C 2
Chipping Sodbury ....**10** B 3
Chollerford ....**20** A 1
Chorley ....**15** D 1
Christchurch ....**5** C 2
Church Stretton ....**10** B 1
Cirencester ....**11** C 3
Clacton-on-Sea ....**13** C 3
Claonaig ....**22** B 2
Clapham (North Yorks.) ......**19** D 3
Clare ....**12** B 3
Claudy ....**46** B 2
Clay Cross ....**16** A 3
Cleethorpes ....**17** C 2
Clevedon ....**4** B 1
Cleveleys ....**15** C 1
Clitheroe ....**15** D 1
Clogh Mills ....**47** C 2
Clovelly ....**3** D 1
Clun ....**10** A 1
Clydebank ....**23** D 2
Coalisland ....**47** C 3
Coalville ....**11** D 1

Coatbridge ....**23** D 2
Cockburnspath ....**24** B 2
Cockermouth ....**19** C 2
Colchester ....**13** C 3
Coldbackie ....**32** A 1
Coldstream ....**24** B 3
Coleford (Glos.) ....**10** B 3
Coleraine ....**47** C 1
Colintraive ....**23** C 2
Colnabaichin ....**29** C 2
Colne ....**15** D 1
Colwyn Bay / Bae Colwyn ...**14** B 2
Combe Martin ....**3** D 1
Comber ....**47** D 3
Congleton ....**15** D 3
Congresbury ....**4** B 1
Conisbrough ....**16** B 3
Coniston ....**19** D 3
Connel ....**23** C 1
Consett ....**20** A 2
Contin ....**28** A 1
Conwy ....**14** B 2
Cookstown ....**47** C 3
Corbridge ....**20** A 2
Corby ....**12** A 2
Corfe Castle ....**5** C 2
Corran ....**27** D 3
Corsham ....**5** C 1
Corwen ....**15** C 3
Cosham ....**5** D 2
Coupar Angus ....**24** A 1
Coventry ....**11** C 1
Cowbridge / Bont-faen ....**9** D 3
Cowdenbeath ....**24** A 2
Cowes (Isle of Wight) ....**5** D 2
Cowfold ....**6** A 2
Craigavon ....**47** C 3
Craigellachie ....**29** C 2
Craighouse ....**22** B 2
Craignure ....**22** B 1
Crail ....**24** B 2
Cranborne ....**5** C 2
Craven Arms ....**10** B 1
Crawley (West Sussex) ....**6** A 2
Creagorry ....**26** B 1
Crediton ....**4** A 2
Crewe ....**15** D 3
Crewkerne ....**4** B 2
Crianlarich ....**23** D 1
Criccieth ....**14** A 3
Crickhowell ....**10** A 3
Cricklade ....**11** C 3
Crieff ....**24** A 1
Crinan ....**22** B 2
Cromarty ....**28** B 1
Cromer ....**13** C 1

Crook ....**20** A 2
Cross Hands ....**9** D 3
Crossmaglen ....**43** C 1
Crowborough ....**6** B 2
Crowland ....**12** A 1
Crowle ....**16** B 2
Croyde ....**3** D 1
Croydon ....**6** B 1
Cruden Bay ....**29** D 2
Crudgington ....**10** B 1
Crumlin ....**47** C 2
Cuckfield ....**6** B 2
Cullen ....**29** C 1
Cullompton ....**4** A 2
Culross ....**24** A 2
Cumbernauld ....**23** D 2
Cumnock ....**23** D 3
Cupar ....**24** B 1
Cushendall ....**47** D 1
Cushendun ....**47** D 1
Cwmbrân ....**10** A 3

D

Dagenham ....**6** B 1
Dalbeattie ....**19** C 1
Dalburgh ....**26** A 2
Dalkeith ....**24** A 2
Dalmally ....**23** C 1
Dalmellington ....**18** B 1
Dalry (North Ayrshire) ....**23** C 3
Dalton in Furness ....**19** C 3
Dalwhinnie ....**28** A 3
Darlington ....**20** B 3
Dartford ....**6** B 1
Dartmouth ....**4** A 3
Darwen ....**15** D 1
Dava ....**28** B 2
Daventry ....**11** D 2
Dawlish ....**4** A 2
Deal ....**7** D 2
Denbigh / Dinbych ....**15** C 2
Dennington ....**13** C 2
Denny ....**23** D 2
Derby ....**16** A 3
Dervaig ....**27** C 3
Desborough ....**11** D 1
Devil's Bridge / Pontarfynach .**9** D 1
Devizes ....**5** C 1
Dewsbury ....**16** A 2
Dingwall ....**28** A 1
Diss ....**13** C 2
Dolgellau ....**14** B 3
Dollar ....**24** A 2
Donaghadee ....**47** D 3
Doncaster ....**16** B 2
Donington ....**12** A 1

Dorchester (*Dorset*) .... 4 B 2
Dorking .... 6 A 2
Dornie .... 27 D 2
Dornoch .... 28 B 1
Douglas (*Isle of Man*) .... 18 B 3
Douglas
  (*South Lanarkshire*) .... 23 D 3
Doune .... 23 D 2
Dover .... 7 D 2
Downham Market .... 12 B 1
Downpatrick .... 47 D 3
Droitwich .... 10 B 2
Dromore (*Down*) .... 47 C 3
Dromore (*Omagh*) .... 46 B 3
Dronfield .... 16 A 2
Drummore .... 18 A 2
Drumnadrochit .... 28 A 2
Dryburgh Abbey .... 24 B 3
Drymen .... 23 D 2
Dufftown .... 29 C 2
Dulnain Bridge .... 28 B 2
Dumbarton .... 23 D 2
Dumfries .... 19 C 1
Dunbar .... 24 B 2
Dunblane .... 23 D 2
Dundee .... 24 B 1
Dundonnell .... 27 D 1
Dunfermline .... 24 A 2
Dungannon .... 46 B 3
Dungiven .... 46 B 2
Dunkeld .... 24 A 1
Dunnamanagh .... 46 B 2
Dunnet .... 33 C 2
Dunoon .... 23 C 2
Duns .... 24 B 3
Dunstable .... 12 A 3
Dunster .... 4 A 1
Dunvegan .... 26 B 1
Durham .... 20 B 2
Durness .... 32 A 2
Dursley .... 10 B 3

E

Eaglescliffe .... 20 B 3
Earith .... 12 B 2
Earlston .... 24 B 3
Easingwold .... 16 B 1
East Dereham .... 13 C 1
East Grinstead .... 6 B 2
East Kilbride .... 23 D 3
East Linton .... 24 B 2
Eastbourne .... 6 B 3
Eastleigh .... 5 D 2
Ebbw Vale / Glyn Ebwy .... 10 A 3
Eccleshall .... 15 D 3
Edinburgh .... 24 A 2

Eglinton .... 46 B 1
Egremont .... 19 C 3
Elgin .... 28 B 1
Elgol .... 27 C 2
Elie .... 24 B 2
Ellesmere .... 15 C 3
Ellesmere Port .... 15 C 2
Ellon .... 29 D 2
Eltisley .... 12 A 2
Elvanfoot .... 24 A 3
Ely .... 12 B 2
Enniskillen .... 46 A 3
Epping .... 6 B 1
Epsom .... 6 A 1
Epworth .... 16 B 2
Esher .... 6 A 1
Ettington .... 11 C 2
Evesham .... 11 C 2
Exeter .... 4 A 2
Exmouth .... 4 A 2
Eye (*Cambs.*) .... 12 A 1
Eyemouth .... 25 C 2

F

Fairford .... 11 C 3
Fakenham .... 13 C 1
Falkirk .... 24 A 2
Falkland .... 24 A 2
Falmouth .... 2 B 3
Fareham .... 5 D 2
Faringdon .... 11 C 3
Farnborough (*Hants.*) .... 6 A 1
Farnham (*Surrey*) .... 6 A 2
Faversham .... 7 C 1
Fawley .... 5 D 2
Felixstowe .... 13 C 3
Felton .... 20 A 1
Feolin Ferry .... 22 B 2
Ffestiniog .... 14 B 3
Filey .... 21 C 3
Finchingfield .... 12 B 3
Fintona .... 46 B 3
Fionnphort .... 22 A 1
Fishbourne .... 5 D 2
Fishguard / Abergwaun .... 9 C 2
Fivemiletown .... 46 B 3
Fleetwood .... 15 C 1
Flint / Fflint .... 15 C 2
Fochabers .... 29 C 1
Folkestone .... 7 C 2
Fordingbridge .... 5 C 2
Forfar .... 24 B 1
Formby Point .... 15 C 2
Forres .... 28 B 1
Fort Augustus .... 28 A 2
Fort William .... 27 D 3

Fortrose .... 28 A 1
Fortuneswell .... 4 B 3
Fowey .... 3 C 3
Foyers .... 28 A 2
Fraddon .... 3 C 3
Fraserburgh .... 29 D 1
Freshwater .... 5 D 2
Frinton-on-Sea .... 13 C 3
Frizington .... 19 C 2
Frodsham .... 15 D 2
Frome .... 4 B 1
Furnace .... 23 C 2

G

Gailey .... 10 B 1
Gainsborough .... 16 B 2
Gairloch .... 27 D 1
Galashiels .... 24 B 3
Galston .... 23 D 3
Garforth .... 16 A 1
Garvagh .... 47 C 2
Garve .... 28 A 1
Garynahine .... 30 B 3
Gatehouse of Fleet .... 18 B 2
Gateshead .... 20 B 2
Gilford .... 47 C 3
Gillingham (*Dorset*) .... 5 C 1
Gillingham (*Kent*) .... 7 C 1
Girvan .... 18 A 1
Gisburn .... 15 D 1
Glamis .... 24 B 1
Glasgow .... 23 D 2
Glastonbury .... 4 B 1
Glenariff or Waterfoot .... 47 D 2
Glenarm .... 47 D 2
Glenelg .... 27 C 2
Glenfinnan .... 27 D 3
Glenluce .... 18 A 1
Glenrothes .... 24 A 2
Glossop .... 16 A 2
Gloucester .... 10 B 3
Godalming .... 6 A 2
Godmanchester .... 12 A 2
Golspie .... 28 B 1
Goole .... 16 B 2
Gorey .... 35 D 2
Gorleston-on-Sea .... 13 D 2
Gortin .... 46 B 3
Gosforth (*Cumbria*) .... 19 C 3
Gosport .... 5 D 2
Gourock .... 23 C 2
Grain .... 7 C 1
Grange-over-Sands .... 19 D 3
Grangemouth .... 24 A 2
Grantham .... 12 A 1
Grantown-on-Spey .... 28 B 2

Grasmere .... 19 D 3
Gravesend .... 6 B 1
Grays Thurrock .... 6 B 1
Great Driffield .... 17 C 1
Great Dunmow .... 12 B 3
Great Malvern .... 10 B 2
Great Torrington .... 3 D 1
Great Yarmouth .... 13 D 1
Greenhead .... 19 D 1
Greenlaw .... 24 B 3
Greenock .... 23 C 2
Greenodd .... 19 D 3
Grey Abbey .... 47 D 3
Grimsby .... 17 C 2
Guildford .... 6 A 1
Guisborough .... 20 B 3
Guist .... 13 C 1
Guyhirn .... 12 B 1

H

Haddington .... 24 B 2
Hadleigh (Suffolk) .... 13 C 3
Hailsham .... 6 B 2
Halesowen .... 11 C 1
Halesworth .... 13 D 2
Halifax .... 16 A 1
Halstead .... 12 B 3
Hamilton .... 23 D 3
Harewood .... 16 A 1
Harlech .... 14 B 3
Harleston .... 13 C 2
Harlow .... 12 B 3
Harpenden .... 12 A 3
Harrogate .... 16 A 1
Hartlepool .... 20 B 2
Harwich .... 13 C 3
Haslemere .... 6 A 2
Hastings .... 7 C 2
Hatfield (Herts.) .... 12 A 3
Hatherleigh .... 3 D 2
Havant .... 5 D 2
Haverfordwest / Hwlffordd ... 8 B 2
Haverhill .... 12 B 3
Hawes .... 20 A 3
Hawick .... 24 B 3
Hawkhurst .... 7 C 2
Hay-on-Wye .... 10 A 2
Hayle .... 2 B 3
Haywards Heath .... 6 B 2
Heanor .... 16 A 3
Heathfield .... 6 B 2
Hedon .... 17 C 1
Helensburgh .... 23 C 2
Helmsdale .... 32 B 3
Helmsley .... 20 B 3
Helston .... 2 B 3

Hemel Hempstead .... 12 A 3
Henley .... 11 C 2
Henley-on-Thames .... 11 D 3
Henstridge .... 4 B 2
Hereford .... 10 B 2
Herne Bay .... 7 C 1
Hertford .... 12 A 3
Hexham .... 20 A 2
Heysham .... 15 C 1
High Wycombe .... 6 A 1
Higham Ferrers .... 12 A 2
Hillswick .... 34 A 1
Hinckley .... 11 C 1
Hindhead .... 6 A 2
Hirwaun .... 9 D 3
Hitchin .... 12 A 3
Hoddesdon .... 12 A 3
Hodnet .... 15 D 2
Holbeach .... 12 B 1
Holmfirth .... 16 A 2
Holsworthy .... 3 D 2
Holt (Norfolk) .... 13 C 1
Holyhead / Caergybi .... 14 A 2
Holywell / Treffynnon .... 15 C 2
Holywood .... 47 D 3
Honiton .... 4 B 2
Horden .... 20 B 2
Horley .... 6 B 2
Horncastle .... 17 C 3
Hornsea .... 17 C 1
Horsham .... 6 A 2
Houghton-le-Spring .... 20 B 2
Hove .... 6 B 2
Howden .... 16 B 1
Hoylake .... 15 C 2
Hucknall .... 16 B 3
Huddersfield .... 16 A 2
Hungerford .... 5 D 1
Hunstanton .... 12 B 1
Huntingdon .... 12 A 2
Huntly .... 29 C 2
Husbands Bosworth .... 11 D 1
Hushinish .... 30 B 3
Hyde .... 15 D 2
Hythe (Kent) .... 7 C 2

I

Ilchester .... 4 B 2
Ilfracombe .... 3 D 1
Ilkeston .... 16 A 3
Ilkley .... 16 A 1
Ilminster .... 4 B 2
Immingham .... 17 C 2
Immingham Dock .... 17 C 2
Inchnadamph .... 32 A 3
Inchree .... 27 D 3

Ingleton (North Yorks.).......... 19 D 3
Innellan .... 23 C 2
Innerleithen .... 24 A 3
Inveraray .... 23 C 1
Inverbervie .... 29 D 3
Invergarry .... 28 A 2
Invergordon .... 28 A 1
Inverkeithing .... 24 A 2
Invermoriston .... 28 A 2
Inverness .... 28 A 2
Inverurie .... 29 D 2
Ipswich .... 13 C 3
Ironbridge .... 10 B 1
Irvine .... 23 C 3
Irvinestown .... 46 A 3
Isbister .... 34 A 1
Isle of Whithorn .... 18 B 2
Isleornsay .... 27 C 2
Ixworth .... 13 C 2

J

Jarrow .... 20 B 2
Jedburgh .... 24 B 3
John o' Groats .... 33 C 2
Johnstone .... 23 D 2

K

Keady .... 47 C 3
Keighley .... 16 A 1
Keith .... 29 C 2
Kelso .... 24 B 3
Kendal .... 19 D 3
Kenilworth .... 11 C 2
Kennacraig .... 22 B 2
Kentallen .... 27 D 3
Kesh .... 46 A 3
Keswick .... 19 D 2
Kettering .... 11 D 2
Keynsham .... 4 B 2
Kidderminster .... 10 B 1
Kidlington .... 11 D 3
Kidsgrove .... 15 D 2
Kidwelly / Cydweli .... 9 C 3
Kilbirnie .... 23 C 3
Kilchoan .... 27 C 3
Kilcreggan .... 23 C 2
Kilkeel .... 43 C 1
Kilkhampton .... 3 C 2
Killin .... 23 D 1
Killyleagh .... 47 D 3
Kilmarnock .... 23 D 3
Kilmartin .... 22 B 2
Kilninver .... 22 B 1
Kilnsea .... 17 C 2
Kilrea .... 47 C 2
Kilsyth .... 23 D 2

Kilwinning .... 23 C 3
Kinbrace .... 32 B 3
Kincardine .... 24 A 2
King's Lynn .... 12 B 1
Kingsbridge .... 3 D 3
Kingston-upon-Hull .... 17 C 1
Kingston-upon-Thames .... 6 A 1
Kingswear .... 4 A 3
Kington .... 10 A 2
Kingussie .... 28 A 3
Kinloch Rannoch .... 28 A 3
Kinlochbervie .... 32 A 2
Kinlochewe .... 27 D 1
Kinross .... 24 A 2
Kintore .... 29 D 2
Kirkby Lonsdale .... 19 D 3
Kirkby Stephen .... 20 A 3
Kirkcaldy .... 24 A 2
Kirkcolm .... 18 A 1
Kirkcudbright .... 18 B 2
Kirkham .... 15 C 1
Kirkintilloch .... 23 D 2
Kirkwall .... 33 C 1
Kirriemuir .... 24 B 1
Knaresborough .... 16 A 1
Knighton / Trefyclawdd .... 10 A 1
Knutsford .... 15 D 2
Kyle of Lochalsh .... 27 C 2
Kyleakin .... 27 C 2
Kylerhea .... 27 C 2
Kylestrome .... 31 D 3

L

Laggan (near Newtonmore).. 28 A 3
Laide .... 27 D 1
Lairg .... 32 A 3
Lamlash .... 23 C 3
Lampeter /
   Llanbedr Pont Steffan ....9 D 2
Lanark .... 23 D 3
Lancaster .... 15 D 1
Lanchester .... 20 A 2
Langholm .... 19 D 1
Langport .... 4 B 1
Largs .... 23 C 2
Larne .... 47 D 2
Latheron .... 32 B 3
Lauder .... 24 B 3
Launceston .... 3 D 2
Laurencekirk .... 29 C 3
Lavenham .... 13 C 3
Laxford Bridge .... 32 A 2
Laxo .... 34 B 2
Leadenham .... 16 B 3
Lechlade .... 11 C 3
Ledbury .... 10 B 2

Ledmore .... 32 A 3
Leeds (West Yorks.)............. 16 A 1
Leek .... 15 D 3
Leicester ....11 D 1
Leighton Buzzard .... 12 A 3
Leiston .... 13 D 2
Leith .... 24 A 2
Leominster .... 10 B 2
Lerwick .... 34 B 2
Letchworth .... 12 A 3
Leuchars .... 24 B 1
Leven
   (East Riding of Yorks.) ..... 17 C 1
Leven (Fife) .... 24 B 2
Leverburgh
   (Isle of Lewis & Harris)...... 26 B 1
Lewes .... 6 B 2
Leyburn .... 20 A 3
Leyland .... 15 D 1
Leysdown-on-Sea ....7 C 1
Lichfield ....11 C 1
Limavady .... 46 B 1
Lincoln .... 17 C 3
Linlithgow .... 24 A 2
Linslade ....11 D 3
Lisburn .... 47 C 3
Liskeard .... 3 C 3
Lisnaskea .... 46 B 3
Littlehampton .... 6 A 3
Littleport .... 12 B 2
Liverpool .... 15 C 2
Livingston .... 24 A 2
Lizard .... 2 B 3
Llanberis .... 14 E 3
Llandeilo ....9 D 2
Llandovery / Llanymddyfri ....9 D 2
Llandrindod Wells ....9 D 2
Llandudno .... 14 B 2
Llandysul ....9 C 2
Llanelli ....9 D 3
Llanerchymedd .... 14 A 2
Llanfairfechan .... 14 B 2
Llanfyllin .... 15 C 3
Llangadog ....9 D 2
Llangefni .... 14 A 2
Llangollen .... 15 C 3
Llangurig ....9 D 1
Llanidloes .... 10 A 1
Llanrhystud ....9 D 1
Llanrwst .... 14 B 3
Llanwrtyd Wells ....9 D 2
Llynclys .... 15 C 3
Loanhead .... 24 A 2
Lochaline .... 22 B 1
Lochboisdale .... 26 A 2
Lochcarron .... 27 D 2

Lochearnhead .... 23 D 1
Lochgelly .... 24 A 2
Lochgilphead .... 22 B 2
Lochinver .... 31 D 3
Lochmaben .... 19 C 1
Lochmaddy .... 26 B 1
Lochranza .... 23 C 3
Lockerbie .... 19 C 1
Loftus .... 20 B 3
London .... 6 B 1
Londonderry .... 46 B 1
Long Eaton .... 16 B 3
Long Preston .... 15 D 1
Long Sutton (Lincs.) .... 12 B 1
Longtown .... 19 D 1
Lopcombe Corner ....5 C 1
Lossiemouth .... 28 B 1
Lostwithiel .... 3 C 3
Loughborough ....11 D 1
Louth .... 17 C 2
Low Street .... 13 D 1
Lowestoft .... 13 D 2
Ludlow .... 10 B 1
Lurgan .... 47 C 3
Luton .... 12 A 3
Lutterworth ....11 D 1
Lydd ....7 C 2
Lydney .... 10 B 3
Lyme Regis .... 4 B 2
Lymington .... 5 D 2
Lyndhurst .... 5 D 2
Lynmouth .... 3 D 1
Lynton .... 3 D 1
Lytham St Anne's .... 15 C 1

M

Mablethorpe .... 17 D 2
Macclesfield .... 15 D 2
Macduff .... 29 C 1
Machrihanish .... 22 B 3
Machynlleth ....9 D 1
Maesteg ....9 D 3
Maghera (Londonderry)........ 47 C 2
Magherafelt .... 47 C 2
Maidenhead .... 6 A 1
Maidstone .... 7 C 2
Maldon .... 12 B 3
Mallaig .... 27 C 3
Mallwyd ....9 D 1
Malmesbury .... 10 B 3
Maltby .... 16 B 2
Malton .... 16 B 1
Manchester .... 15 D 2
Mansfield .... 16 B 3
March .... 12 B 2
Margate ....7 D 1

Market Drayton	15	D 3
Market Harborough	11	D 1
Market Rasen	17	C 2
Market Weighton	16	B 1
Markethill	47	C 3
Marlborough	5	C 1
Marlow	6	A 1
Marske-by-the-Sea	20	B 2
Marykirk	29	C 3
Maryport	19	C 2
Matlock	16	A 3
Mauchline	23	D 3
Maypole	23	C 3
Meigle	24	A 1
Melksham	5	C 1
Melrose	24	B 3
Melton Mowbray	11	D 1
Melvich	32	B 2
Menai Bridge /		
Porthaethwy	14	B 2
Mere (Wilts.)	5	C 1
Merthyr Tydfil	10	A 3
Methil	24	B 2
Mevagissey	3	C 3
Mid Yell	34	B 1
Middlesbrough	20	B 2
Middleton-in-Teesdale	20	A 2
Middlewich	15	D 3
Midhurst	6	A 2
Milford	6	A 2
Milford Haven /		
Aberdaugleddau	8	B 3
Millom	19	C 3
Millport	23	C 2
Milton Keynes	11	D 2
Minehead	4	A 1
Minsterley	10	A 1
Mintlaw	29	D 2
Modbury	3	D 3
Moffat	19	C 1
Mold / Yr Wyddgrug	15	C 3
Moneymore	47	C 2
Monifieth	24	B 1
Monmouth / Trefynwy	10	B 3
Montgomery / Trefaldwyn	10	A 1
Montrose	24	B 1
Morecambe	15	D 1
Moreton-in-Marsh	11	C 2
Moretonhampstead	3	D 2
Morpeth	20	A 1
Mossat	29	C 2
Motherwell	23	D 3
Mountain Ash /		
Aberpennar	10	A 3
Much Wenlock	10	B 1
Muir of Ord	28	A 1

Muirkirk	23	D 3
Mumbles (The)	9	D 3
Mundesley	13	C 1
Mundford	12	B 2
Musselburgh	24	A 2

N

Nailsworth	10	B 3
Nairn	28	B 1
Nantwich	15	D 3
Narberth / Arberth	9	C 3
Neath / Castell-nedd	9	D 3
Nefyn	14	A 3
Nelson	15	D 1
New Abbey	19	C 1
New Alresford	5	D 1
New Cumnock	23	D 3
New Deer	29	D 2
New Galloway	18	B 1
New Quay / Ceinewydd	9	C 2
New Romney	7	C 2
Newark-on-Trent	16	B 3
Newbiggin-by-the-Sea	20	B 1
Newborough	14	A 2
Newburgh		
(Aberdeenshire)	29	D 2
Newburgh (Fife)	24	A 1
Newbury	5	D 1
Newcastle (Down)	47	D 3
Newcastle Emlyn /		
Castell Newydd Emlyn	9	C 2
Newcastle-under-Lyme	15	D 3
Newcastle-upon-Tyne	20	B 2
Newhaven	6	B 3
Newmarket (Suffolk)	12	B 2
Newnham (Glos.)	10	B 3
Newport (I.O.W.)	5	D 2
Newport (Pembrokes)	9	C 2
Newport (Salop)	10	B 1
Newport /		
Casnewydd (Newport)	10	A 3
Newport-on-Tay	24	B 1
Newport Pagnell	11	D 2
Newquay	2	B 3
Newry	47	B 3
Newton Abbot	4	A 2
Newton-Aycliffe	20	B 2
Newton Ferrers	3	D 3
Newton Stewart	18	B 1
Newtonmore	28	A 3
Newtown (Heref.)	10	B 3
Newtown / Drenewydd		
(Powys)	10	A 1
Newtown St Boswells	24	A 3
Newtownabbey	47	D 2
Newtownards	47	D 3

Newtownbutler	46	B 3
Newtownhamilton	47	C 3
Newtownstewart	46	B 2
Neyland	9	C 3
Niton	5	D 3
North Berwick	24	A 2
North Walsham	13	C 1
Northallerton	20	B 3
Northam	3	D 1
Northampton	11	D 2
Northleach	11	C 3
Northwich	15	D 3
Norton	16	B 1
Norwich	13	C 1
Nottingham	16	B 3
Nuneaton	11	C 1

O

Oadby	11	D 1
Oakham	11	D 1
Oban	22	B 1
Okehampton	3	D 2
Oldham	15	D 2
Oldmeldrum	29	D 2
Ollerton	16	B 3
Omagh	46	B 2
Onich	27	D 3
Ormskirk	15	C 2
Orpington	6	B 1
Orton	19	D 3
Oswestry	15	C 3
Othery	4	B 1
Otley (West Yorks.)	16	A 1
Otter Ferry	23	C 2
Otterburn	20	A 1
Ottery St Mary	4	A 2
Oundle	12	A 2
Outwell	12	B 1
Oxford	11	D 3

P

Padiham	15	D 1
Padstow	3	C 2
Paignton	4	A 3
Painswick	10	B 3
Paisley	23	D 2
Pangbourne-on-Thames	5	D 1
Partney	17	C 3
Pateley Bridge	16	A 1
Patrington	17	C 2
Patterdale	19	D 2
Peebles	24	A 3
Peel	18	A 3
Pembroke / Penfro	9	C 3
Pembroke Dock /		
Doc Penfro	9	C 3

Penarth	10	A 3
Pendine	9	C 3
Penicuik	24	A 2
Penmaenmawr	14	B 2
Penrhyndeudraeth	14	B 3
Penrith	19	D 2
Penryn	2	B 3
Pentrefoelas	14	B 3
Penzance	2	B 3
Pershore	11	C 2
Perth	24	A 1
Peterborough	12	A 2
Peterhead	29	D 2
Peterlee	20	B 2
Petersfield	5	D 2
Petworth	6	A 2
Pewsey	5	C 1
Pickering	21	C 3
Pierowall	33	C 1
Pitlochry	28	B 3
Pittenween	24	B 2
Plumbridge	46	B 2
Plymouth	3	D 3
Plympton	3	D 3
Plymstock	3	D 3
Polegate	6	B 2
Polperro	3	C 3
Pontardawe	9	D 3
Pontarddulais	9	D 3
Pontefract	16	B 2
Pontrilas	10	A 2
Pontypool / Pontypwl	10	A 3
Pontypridd	10	A 3
Poole	5	C 2
Porlock	4	A 1
Port Askaig	22	B 2
Port Charlotte	22	A 2
Port Ellen	22	A 3
Port Erin	18	A 3
Port-Eynon	9	C 3
Port Glasgow	23	C 2
Port of Ness	31	C 2
Port St Mary	18	A 3
Port Talbot	9	D 3
Port William	18	B 2
Portadown	47	C 3
Portaferry	47	D 3
Portavogie	47	D 3
Portglenone	47	C 2
Porthcawl	9	D 3
Porthmadog	14	B 3
Portishead	10	A 3
Portnacroish	23	C 1
Portnaguran	31	C 3
Portnahaven	22	A 2
Portpatrick	18	A 2

Portree	27	C 2
Portrush	47	C 1
Portsmouth	5	D 2
Portstewart	47	C 1
Potters Bar	6	B 1
Potton	12	A 3
Prestatyn	15	C 2
Presteigne	10	A 2
Preston (*Lancs.*)	15	D 1
Prestonpans	24	B 2
Prestwick	23	C 2
Princetown	3	D 2
Prudhoe	20	A 2
Puckeridge	12	A 3
Pulborough	6	A 2
Pwllheli	14	A 3

Q

Queenborough	7	C 1
Queensferry	15	C 2

R

Radstock	4	B 1
Raglan	10	A 3
Ramsey (*Cambs.*)	12	A 2
Ramsey (*Isle of Man*)	18	B 3
Ramsgate	7	D 1
Randalstown	47	C 2
Rathfriland	47	C 3
Rattray	24	A 1
Rawtenstall	15	D 1
Rayleigh	7	C 1
Reading	5	D 1
Redcar	20	B 2
Redditch	11	C 2
Redhill	6	B 2
Redruth	2	B 3
Reeth	20	A 3
Reigate	6	A 2
Reiss	33	C 2
Rempstone	11	D 1
Retford	16	B 2
Rhayader / Rhaeadr	10	A 2
Rhondda	10	A 3
Rhosneigr	14	A 2
Rhossili	9	C 3
Rhyl	15	C 2
Rhynie	29	C 2
Richmond	20	A 3
Richmond-upon-Thames	6	A 1
Ringford	18	B 2
Ringwood	5	C 2
Ripley (*Derbs.*)	16	A 2
Ripon	20	B 3
Risca	10	A 3
Roadside	32	B 2

Rochdale	15	D 2
Rochester	7	C 1
Rodel	26	B 1
Romsey	5	D 2
Ross-on-Wye	10	B 2
Rosslea	46	B 3
Rosthwaite	19	D 2
Rostrevor	43	C 1
Rothbury	20	A 1
Rotherham	16	A 2
Rothes	29	C 2
Rothesay	23	C 2
Rothwell (*Northants.*)	11	D 1
Royal Leamington Spa	11	C 2
Royal Tunbridge Wells	6	B 2
Royston (*Herts.*)	12	A 3
Ruabon	15	C 3
Rugby	11	D 2
Rugeley	11	C 1
Runcorn	15	D 2
Rushden	12	A 2
Ruthin / Rnuthun	15	C 3
Ryde (*Isle of Wight*)	5	D 2
Rye Foreign	7	C 2

S

Saffron Walden	12	B 3
St Albans	12	A 3
St Andrews	24	B 1
St Asaph	15	C 2
St Austell	3	C 3
St Clears / Sanclêr	9	C 2
St David's / Tyddewi	8	B 2
St Helens (*Merseyside*)	15	D 2
St Helier (*Jersey*)	35	D 2
St Ives (*Cambs.*)	12	A 2
St Ives (*Cornwall*)	2	B 3
St Just	2	B 3
St Keverne	2	B 3
St Mawes	3	C 3
St Monans	24	B 2
St Neots	12	A 2
St Peter Port (*Guernsey*)	35	C 1
Saintfield	47	D 3
Salcombe	3	D 3
Salen (*Argyll and Bute*)	22	B 1
Salen (*Highland*)	27	C 3
Salisbury	5	C 1
Saltash	3	D 3
Saltburn-by-the-Sea	20	B 2
Saltcoats	23	C 3
Sandbach	15	D 3
Sandness	34	A 2
Sandown	5	D 2
Sandwich	7	D 2
Sandy	12	A 3

Sanquhar	23	D 3
Saundersfoot	9	C 3
Sawbridgeworth	12	B 3
Saxmundham	13	C 2
Scalasaig	22	A 2
Scalby	21	C 3
Scalloway	34	B 2
Scarborough	21	C 3
Scarinish	22	A 1
Scole	13	C 2
Sconser	27	C 2
Scourie	31	D 3
Scrabster	32	B 2
Scunthorpe	16	B 2
Seaford	6	B 3
Seaham	20	B 2
Seaton	4	A 2
Seaton Delaval	20	B 1
Sedbergh	19	D 3
Sedgefield	20	B 2
Selby	16	B 1
Selkirk	24	B 3
Selsey	6	A 3
Sennen	2	B 3
Sennybridge	9	D 2
Settle	15	D 1
Sevenoaks	6	B 1
Shaftesbury	5	C 2
Shanklin	5	D 2
Shap	19	D 3
Sheerness	7	C 1
Sheffield	16	A 2
Shefford	12	A 3
Shepshed	11	D 1
Shepton Mallet	4	B 1
Sherborne	4	B 2
Sheringham	13	C 1
Shiel Bridge	27	D 2
Shieldaig	27	D 1
Shipston-on-Stour	11	C 2
Shoreham	6	A 2
Shrewsbury	10	B 1
Shrewton	5	C 1
Sidmouth	4	A 2
Silloth	19	C 2
Simonsbath	4	A 1
Sittingbourne	7	C 1
Skaill	33	C 1
Skegness	17	D 3
Skelmersdale	15	D 2
Skipton	16	A 1
Sleaford	12	A 1
Sligachan (Loch)	27	C 2
Slough	6	A 1
Snaith	16	B 2
Soham	12	B 2
Solihull	11	C 1
South Molton	3	D 1
South Queensferry	24	A 2
South Shields	20	B 2
Southam	11	D 2
Southampton	5	D 2
Southborough	6	B 2
Southend	22	B 3
Southend-on-Sea	7	C 1
Southport	15	C 1
Southsea	5	D 2
Southwell	16	B 3
Southwold	13	C 2
Spalding	12	A 1
Spean Bridge	27	D 3
Spennymoor	20	B 2
Spilsby	17	C 3
Staffin	27	C 1
Stafford	15	D 3
Staines	6	A 1
Stamford	12	A 1
Stanley (Durham)	20	A 2
Stansted Mountfitchet	12	B 3
Staveley (Derbs.)	16	A 2
Stenness (Orkney Islands)	33	C 1
Stevenage	12	A 3
Stewarton	23	D 3
Stirling	23	D 2
Stockbridge	5	D 1
Stockport	15	D 2
Stocksbridge	16	A 2
Stockton-on-Tees	20	B 3
Stoke-on-Trent	15	D 3
Stone (Staffs.)	15	D 3
Stonehaven	29	D 3
Stornoway	31	C 3
Stourbridge	10	B 1
Stourport-on-Severn	10	B 2
Stow-on-the-Wold	11	C 2
Stowmarket	13	C 2
Strabane	46	B 2
Stradsett	12	B 1
Strangford	47	D 3
Stranraer	18	A 1
Stratford-upon-Avon	11	C 2
Strathaven	23	D 3
Stratton (Cornwall)	3	C 2
Streatley	11	D 3
Street	4	B 1
Stromeferry	27	D 2
Stromness	33	C 1
Strontian	27	C 3
Stroud	10	B 3
Sturminster Newton	5	C 2
Sudbury (Derbs.)	16	A 3
Sudbury (Suffolk)	12	B 3
Sumburgh	34	B 3
Sunderland	20	B 2
Sutterton	12	A 1
Sutton (London Borough)	6	A 1
Sutton Coldfield	11	C 1
Sutton-in-Ashfield	16	B 3
Sutton-on-Sea	17	B 2
Swadlincote	11	C 1
Swaffham	12	B 1
Swanage	5	C 2
Swanley	6	B 1
Swansea / Abertawe	9	D 3
Swindon	11	C 3
Synod Inn	9	C 2
Syre	32	A 2

T

Tadcaster	16	B 1
Tain	28	B 1
Talgarth	10	A 2
Tamworth	11	C 1
Tandragee	47	C 3
Tarbert (Argyll and Bute)	22	B 3
Tarbert (Western Isles)	30	B 3
Tarbet	23	C 2
Tarporley	15	D 3
Taunton	4	A 1
Tavistock	3	D 2
Tayinloan	22	B 3
Taynuilt	23	C 1
Tayport	24	B 1
Tebay	19	D 3
Teignmouth	4	A 2
Telford	10	B 1
Tenbury Wells	10	B 2
Tenby / Dinbych-y-pysgod	9	C 3
Tenterden	7	C 2
Tetbury	10	B 3
Tewkesbury	10	B 2
Thame	11	D 3
Thetford	13	C 2
Thirsk	20	B 3
Thorne	16	B 2
Thornhill (Dumfries and Galloway)	19	C 1
Thrapston	12	A 2
Threshfield	16	A 1
Thursby	19	D 2
Thurso	32	B 2
Tigharry	26	A 1
Tighnabruaich	23	C 2
Tilbury	6	B 1
Tintagel	3	C 2
Tiverton	4	A 2
Tobermore	47	C 2
Tobermory	27	C 3

Toberonochy	22	B 1
Todmorden	15	D 1
Toft	34	B 1
Tomintoul	28	B 2
Tonbridge	6	B 2
Tongue	32	A 2
Tore	28	A 1
Torpoint	3	A 3
Torquay	4	A 3
Torridon	27	D 1
Totnes	3	D 3
Towcester	11	D 2
Tranent	24	B 2
Tredegar	10	A 3
Tregaron	9	D 2
Tregony	3	C 3
Tring	11	D 3
Troon	23	C 3
Trowbridge	5	C 1
Truro	2	B 3
Turnberry	18	A 1
Turriff	29	C 2
Tuxford	15	D 2
Tyndrum	23	C 1
Tynemouth	20	B 1
Tywyn	9	D 1

U

Uckfield	6	B 2
Uig *(Highland)*	27	C 1
Ullapool	27	D 1
Ulsta	34	B 1
Ulverston	19	D 3
Upavon	5	C 1
Uppingham	11	D 1
Upton-upon-Severn	10	B 2
Usk / Brynbuga	10	A 3
Uttoxeter	16	A 3

V

Ventnor	5	D 3
Voe	34	B 2

W

Wadebridge	3	C 2
Wakefield	16	A 2
Wallasey	15	C 2
Wallingford	11	D 3
Walls	34	A 2
Walsall	11	C 1
Walton-on-the-Naze	13	C 3
Wantage	11	C 3
Ware	12	A 3
Wareham	5	C 2
Warkworth	20	B 1

Warminster	5	C 1
Warrenpoint	43	C 1
Warrington	15	D 2
Warwick	11	C 2
Washington (Tyne and Wear)	20	B 2
Watchet	4	A 1
Watford	6	A 1
Watton	13	C 2
Weldon	12	A 2
Wellingborough	11	D 2
Wellington *(Somerset)*	4	A 2
Wells	4	B 1
Wells-next-the-Sea	13	C 1
Welshpool / Trallwng	10	A 1
Welwyn Garden City	12	A 3
Wem	15	C 3
Wemyss Bay	23	C 2
West Auckland	20	A 2
West Bridgford	16	B 3
West Kilbride	23	C 3
West Linton	24	A 3
West Looe	3	C 3
West Mersea	13	C 3
Westbury *(Wilts.)*	5	C 1
Weston-super-Mare	4	B 1
Wetherby	16	A 1
Wetwang	17	C 1
Weyhill	5	D 1
Weymouth	4	B 2
Whaley Bridge	16	A 2
Whitburn *(West Lothian)*	24	A 2
Whitby	21	C 3
Whitchurch	15	D 3
Whitebridge	28	A 2
Whitehaven	19	C 2
Whitehead	47	D 2
Whiteness	34	B 2
Whithorn	18	B 2
Whitland	9	C 2
Whitley Bay	20	B 1
Whitstable	7	C 1
Whittlesey	12	A 2
Wick *(Highland)*	33	C 3
Wickford	7	C 1
Widnes	15	D 2
Wigan	15	D 2
Wigton	19	D 2
Wigtown	18	B 2
Williton	4	A 1
Wilmslow	15	D 2
Wilton	5	C 1
Wimborne Minster	5	C 2
Wincanton	4	B 1
Winchcombe	11	C 3
Winchelsea	7	C 2

Winchester	5	D 1
Windermere	19	D 3
Windsor	6	A 1
Winkleigh	3	D 2
Winsford *(Cheshire)*	15	D 3
Wisbech	12	B 1
Wishaw	23	D 3
Witham	12	B 3
Withernsea	17	C 1
Witney	11	C 3
Woburn	11	D 2
Woking	6	A 1
Wokingham	6	A 1
Wolsingham	20	A 2
Wolverhampton	10	B 1
Wolverton	11	D 2
Woodbridge	13	C 3
Woodhall Spa	17	C 3
Woodstock	11	D 3
Wooler	25	C 3
Worcester	10	B 2
Workington	19	C 2
Worksop	16	B 2
Worthing	6	A 2
Wragby	17	C 3
Wrexham / Wrecsam	15	C 3
Wroughton	11	C 3
Wymondham *(Norfolk)*	13	C 2

Y

Yarmouth	5	D 2
Yeovil	4	B 2
York	16	B 1
Yoxford	13	D 2

A

Abbeyfeale .... **37** **C 1**
Abbeyleix / Mainistir Laoise . **42** **A 3**
Adare .... **37** **C 1**
Anascaul .... **36** **A 1**
Ardara .... **45** **D 2**
Ardee / Baile Átha Fhirdhia .. **43** **C 1**
Ardmore / Aird Mhór .... **38** **C 2**
Ardrahan .... **41** **C 2**
Arklow / An tInbhear Mór ..... **39** **C 1**
Arthurstown .... **38** **B 2**
Ashbourne .... **43** **C 2**
Askeaton .... **37** **C 1**
Athboy .... **42** **B 2**
Athenry / Baile Átha an Rí ... **41** **D 2**
Athlone / Baile Átha Luain ... **42** **A 2**
Athy / Baile Átha Í .... **42** **B 3**
Aughrim (Wicklow)............... **43** **C 3**

B

Bagenalstown / Muine Bheag **38** **B 1**
Bailieborough /
    Coill an Chollaigh .... **42** **B 1**
Balbriggan / Baile Brigín ...... **43** **C 2**
Ballina / Béal an Átha .... **45** **C 3**
Ballinamore /
    Béal an Átha Mhóir .... **42** **A 1**
Ballinasloe /
    Béal Átha na Sluaighe ..... **41** **D 2**
Ballingarry (Tipperary) .... **38** **A 1**
Ballinrobe / Baile an Róba ... **41** **C 1**
Ballintubber .... **41** **C 1**
Ballybay .... **42** **B 1**
Ballybofey / Bealach Féich ... **46** **A 2**
Ballybunnion .... **36** **B 1**
Ballycastle (Mayo) .... **45** **C 3**
Ballyconnell .... **46** **A 3**
Ballycotton .... **37** **D 3**
Ballycroy .... **44** **B 3**
Ballyduff (Kerry).................. **36** **B 1**
Ballyforan .... **41** **D 2**
Ballyhaunis /
    Béal Átha hAmhnais .... **41** **D 1**
Ballyheige .... **36** **B 1**
Ballyjamesduff .... **42** **B 1**
Ballymahon /
    Baile Uí Mhatháin .... **42** **A 2**
Ballymoe .... **41** **D 1**
Ballymore .... **42** **A 2**
Ballymote / Baile an Mhóta .. **45** **D 3**

Ballysadare .... **45** **D 3**
Ballyshannon /
    Béal Átha Seanaidh .... **46** **A 2**
Ballyvaughan .... **41** **C 2**
Baltinglass /
    Bealach Conglais .... **42** **B 3**
Banagher .... **42** **A 2**
Bandon /
    Droichead na Bandan .... **37** **C 3**
Bangor (Mayo) .... **45** **C 3**
Bantry / Beanntraí .... **36** **B 3**
Barna / Bearna .... **41** **C 2**
Belmullet /
    Béal an Mhuirthead .... **44** **B 3**
Belturbet / Béal Tairbirt .... **46** **A 3**
Birr / Biorra .... **42** **A 3**
Blackwater .... **39** **C 1**
Blarney .... **37** **C 2**
Boherbue .... **37** **C 2**
Borris .... **38** **B 1**
Borrisokane /
    Buiríos Uí Chéin .... **41** **D 3**
Boyle / Mainistir na Búille .... **41** **D 1**
Bray / Bré .... **43** **C 3**
Broadford (Clare)................. **41** **D 3**
Bunclody .... **38** **B 1**
Buncrana / Bun Cranncha ... **46** **B 1**
Bundoran / Bun Dobhráin ... **46** **A 3**
Bunmahon .... **38** **A 2**
Buttevant .... **37** **C 1**

C

Caher / An Chathair .... **37** **D 1**
Cahersiveen /
    Cathair Saidhbhín .... **36** **A 2**
Callan / Callainn .... **38** **A 1**
Cappoquin /
    Ceapach Choinn .... **37** **D 2**
Carlingford .... **43** **C 1**
Carlow / Ceatharlach .... **42** **B 3**
Carna .... **40** **B 2**
Carndonagh /
    Carn Domhnach .... **46** **B 1**
Carnew .... **38** **B 1**
Carrick-on-Shannon-
    Cora Droma Rúisc .... **42** **A 1**
Carrick-on-Suir /
    Carraig na Siúire .... **38** **A 1**
Carrickmacross /
    Carraig Mhachaire Rois ... **42** **B 1**
Carrigart / Carraig Airt .... **46** **A 1**

Cashel / Caiseal (Tipperary) . **37** **D 1**
Castlepollard .... **42** **B 1**
Castlebar /
    Caisleán an Bharraigh .... **41** **C 1**
Castlebellingham .... **43** **C 1**
Castleblayney /
    Baile na Lorgan .... **42** **B 1**
Castlecomer /
    Caisleán an Chomair ...... **42** **A 3**
Castledermot .... **42** **B 3**
Castleisland /
    Oileán Ciarraí .... **36** **B 1**
Castlemaine .... **36** **B 1**
Castlerea /
    An Caisleán Riabhach .... **41** **D 1**
Castletownbere .... **36** **A 3**
Cavan / An Cabhán .... **42** **B 1**
Ceanannus Mór (Kells) /
    Ceananas .... **42** **B 1**
Charlestown (Mayo) .... **41** **D 1**
Charleville / An Ráth .... **37** **C 1**
Clara / Clóirtheach
    (Offaly) .... **42** **A 2**
Claremorris /
    Clár Chlainne Mhuiris .... **41** **C 1**
Clifden / An Clochán .... **40** **B 1**
Cloghan (Offaly) .... **42** **A 2**
Clogheen .... **37** **D 2**
Clogherhead .... **43** **C 1**
Clonakilty /
    Cloich na Coillte .... **37** **C 3**
Clonbur / An Fhairche .... **41** **C 1**
Clondalkin .... **43** **C 2**
Clones / Cluain Eois .... **46** **B 3**
Clonmel / Cluain Meala ...... **38** **A 1**
Coachford .... **37** **C 2**
Cobh / An Cóbh .... **37** **D 2**
Cong / Conga .... **41** **C 1**
Cootehill / Muinchille .... **42** **B 1**
Cork / Corcaigh .... **37** **C 2**
Corrofin .... **41** **C 2**
Courtown .... **39** **C 1**
Craughwell .... **41** **D 2**
Creegh .... **40** **B 3**
Creeslough .... **46** **A 1**
Crolly / Croithlí .... **46** **A 1**
Croom .... **37** **C 1**
Crosshaven .... **37** **D 3**
Crossmolina /
    Crois Mhaoilíona .... **45** **C 3**
Culdaff .... **46** **B 1**

D

Dalkey	43	C 3
Delvin	42	B 2
Dingle / An Daingean	36	A 1
Dolla	41	D 3
Donegal / Dún na nGall	46	A 2
Dowra	46	A 3
Drogheda / Droichead Átha	43	C 2
Dromcolliher	37	C 1
Drumkeeran	46	A 3
Drumshanbo	42	A 1
Dublin / Baile Átha Cliath	43	C 2
Duleek	43	C 2
Dun Laoghaire	43	C 3
Dundalk / Dún Dealgan	43	C 1
Dunfanaghy	46	A 1
Dungarvan / Dún Garbhán	38	A 2
Dunglow / An Clochán Liath	46	A 1
Dunmanway / Dún Mánmhaí	37	C 3
Dunmore / Dún Mór	41	D 1
Dunmore East	38	B 2
Dunshaughlin	43	C 2
Durrow	42	A 3

E

Easky	45	D 3
Édenderry / Éadan Doire	42	B 2
Edgeworthstown / Meathas Troim	42	A 1
Elphin	41	D 1
Ennis / Inis	41	C 3
Enniscorthy / Inis Córthaidh	38	B 1
Enniskerry	43	C 3
Ennistimon / Inis Díomáin	41	C 3

F

Ferbane	42	A 2
Fermoy / Mainistir Fhear Maí	37	D 2
Fethard / Fiodh Ard (Tipperary)	38	A 1
Fintown / Baile na Finne	46	A 2
Foxford	45	C 3
Frenchpark	41	D 1
Freshford	38	A 1

G

Galway / Gaillimh	41	C 2
Glenamoy / Gleann na Muaidhe	45	C 3
Glenbeigh	36	B 2
Glencolumbkille / Gleann Cholm Cille	45	D 2
Glendalough	43	C 3
Glengarriff / An Gleann Garbh	36	B 2
Glennamaddy	41	D 1
Glenties	46	A 2
Gorey / Guaire	39	C 1
Gort / An Gort	41	C 3
Gorteen	41	D 1
Gortmore / An Gort Mór	40	B 2
Graiguenamanagh / Graig na Manach	38	B 1
Gránard / Granard	42	A 1
Greystones / Na Clocha Liatha	43	C 3

H

Headford / Áth Cinn	41	C 2
Hollywood	42	B 2
Holy Cross	38	A 1
Hospital	37	D 1
Howth / Binn Éadair	43	C 2

I

Inishcrone	45	C 3
Innfield	42	B 2

K

Kanturk / Ceann Toirc	37	C 2
Keadew	46	A 3
Keel	44	B 3
Kenmare / Neidín	36	B 2
Kilbaha	40	B 3
Kilbeggan	42	A 2
Kilcock	42	B 2
Kilcormac	42	A 3
Kilcullen	42	B 3
Kildare / Cill Dara	42	B 3
Kildorrery	37	D 1
Kilfenora	41	C 3
Kilgarvan	36	B 2
Kilkee / Cill Chaoi	40	B 3
Kilkenny / Cill Chainnigh	38	A 1
Killadysert	41	C 3
Killaloe / Cill Dalua	41	D 3
Killarney / Cill Airne	36	B 2
Killashandra	42	A 1
Killenaule	38	A 1
Killimer	40	B 3
Killorglin / Cill Orglan	36	B 2
Killybegs / Na Cealla Beaga	45	D 2
Kilmaine	41	C 1
Kilmallock / Cill Mocheallóg	37	D 1
Kilmore Quay	38	B 2
Kilmurry *(near Kilkishen)*	41	C 3
Kilronan / Cill Rónáin	40	B 2
Kilrush / Cill Rois	40	B 3
Kiltealy	38	B 1
Kiltimagh	41	C 1
Kingscourt	42	B 1
Kinnegad	42	B 2
Kinnitty	42	A 3
Kinsale / Cionn tSáile	37	C 3
Kinvarra	41	C 2
Knight's Town	36	A 2

L

Labasheeda	41	C 3
Lahinch / An Leacht	41	C 3
Lanesborough	42	A 1
Laragh	43	C 3
Lauragh	36	B 2
Leenane	40	B 1
Letterfrack	40	B 1
Letterkenny / Leitir Ceanainn	46	A 1
Lettermullan / Leitir Mealláin	40	B 2
Lifford	46	B 2
Limerick / Luimneach	37	D 1
Lisdoonvarna / Lios Dúin Bhearna	41	C 3
Lismore / Lios Mór	37	D 2
Listowel / Lios Tuathail	36	B 1
Longford / An Longfort (Longford)	42	A 1
Loughrea / Baile Locha Riach	41	D 2
Louisburgh	40	B 1
Lucan	43	C 2
Lusk	43	C 2

M

Maam Cross / An Teach Dóite	41	C 2
Macroom / Maigh Chromtha	37	C 2
Malahide / Mullach Íde	43	C 2
Mallow / Mala	37	C 2
Manorhamilton / Cluainín	46	A 3
Maynooth / Maigh Nuad	42	B 2
Midleton / Maiaistir na Corann	37	D 2
Milestone	37	D 1

Millford .... **46** **A 1**
Millstreet .... **37** **C 2**
Milltown Malbay /
   Sráid na Cathrach .... **41** **C 3**
Mitchelstown /
   Baile Mhistéala .... **37** **D 1**
Moate / An Móta .... **42** **A 2**
Mohill / Maothail .... **42** **A 1**
Monaghan / Muineachán ...... **46** **B 3**
Monasterevin .... **42** **B 3**
Moneygall .... **41** **D 3**
Mount Bellew / An Creagán . **41** **D 2**
Mountmellick /
   Móinteach Milic .... **42** **A 3**
Mountrath .... **42** **A 3**
Moville / Bun an Phobail ...... **46** **B 1**
Muff .... **46** **B 1**
Mullingar /
   An Muileann gCearr .... **42** **A 2**
Mulrany / An Mhala Raithní . **44** **B 3**

N

Naas / An Nás .... **42** **B 3**
Naul .... **43** **C 2**
Navan / An Uaimh .... **42** **B 2**
Nenagh / An tAonach .... **41** **D 3**
New Ross /
   Ros Mhic Thriúin .... **38** **B 1**
Newbridge /
   An Droichead Nua .... **42** **B 3**
Newcastle West /
   An Caisleán Nua .... **37** **C 1**
Newmarket .... **37** **C 1**
Newmarket on Fergus .... **41** **C 3**
Newport *(Tipperary)* .... **41** **D 3**
Newport /
   Baile Uí Fhiacháin *(Mayo)* **41** **C 1**

O

Oldcastle /
   An Seanchaisleán .... **42** **B 1**
Oranmore .... **41** **C 2**
Oughterard / Uachtar Ard .... **41** **C 2**

P

Pettigoe .... **46** **A 2**
Pontoon .... **45** **C 3**
Portarlington /
   Cúil an tSúdaire .... **42** **B 3**
Portlaoise / Port Laoise .... **42** **A 3**
Portmarnock .... **43** **C 2**

Portsalon .... **46** **B 1**
Portumna / Port Omna .... **41** **D 3**

Q

Quigley's Point .... **46** **B 1**

R

Rathdowney .... **42** **A 3**
Rathdrum / Ráth Droma ...... **43** **C 3**
Rathkeale / Ráth Caola .... **37** **C 1**
Rathmelton .... **46** **A 1**
Rathmore .... **37** **C 2**
Rathmullan .... **46** **B 1**
Rathnew .... **43** **C 3**
Ringaskiddy .... **37** **D 2**
Roscommon /
   Ros Comáin .... **41** **D 1**
Roscrea / Ros Cré .... **42** **A 3**
Rosscarbery .... **37** **C 3**
Rosses Point .... **45** **D 3**
Rosslare / Ros Láir .... **38** **B 2**
Rosslare Harbour /
   Calafort Ros Láir .... **39** **C 2**
Roundstone .... **40** **B 2**
Rush / An Ros .... **43** **C 2**

S

Scarriff / An Scairbh .... **41** **D 3**
Shercock .... **42** **B 1**
Skerries / Na Sceirí .... **43** **C 2**
Skibbereen / An Sciobairín .. **36** **B 3**
Skull / Schull .... **36** **B 3**
Slane .... **43** **C 2**
Sligo / Sligeach .... **45** **D 3**
Sneem .... **36** **B 2**
Spiddal / An Spidéal .... **41** **C 2**
Strandhill .... **45** **D 3**
Stranorlar .... **46** **A 2**
Strokestown .... **42** **A 1**
Swanlinbar .... **46** **A 3**
Swinford /
   Béal Atha na Muice .... **41** **C 1**
Swords / Sord .... **43** **C 2**

T

Tallow .... **37** **D 2**
Tarbert .... **36** **B 1**
Templemore /
   An Teampall Mór .... **42** **A 3**
Thomastown /
   Baile Mhic Andáin .... **38** **B 1**

Thurles / Durlas .... **38** **A 1**
Timoleague .... **37** **C 3**
Tinahely .... **38** **B 1**
Tipperary / Tiobraid Árann ... **37** **D 1**
Tralee / Trá Lí .... **36** **B 1**
Tramore / Trá Mhór .... **38** **A 2**
Trim / Baile Átha Troim .... **42** **B 2**
Tuam / Tuaim .... **41** **C 2**
Tubbercurry /
   Tobar an Choire .... **45** **D 3**
Tulla .... **41** **C 3**
Tullamore / Tulach Mhór ..... **42** **A 2**
Tullow / An Tulach .... **38** **B 1**
Tulsk .... **41** **D 1**

U

Urlingford .... **38** **A 1**

V

Virginia .... **42** **B 1**

W

Waterford / Port Láirge .... **38** **A 2**
Waterville / An Coireán .... **36** **A 2**
Wellington Bridge .... **38** **B 2**
Westport / Cathair na Mart .. **41** **C 1**
Wexford / Loch Garman ...... **38** **B 2**
Wicklow / Cill Mhantáin .... **43** **C 3**

Y

Youghal / Eochaill .... **37** **D 2**

Dressée par la Manufacture Française des Pneumatiques MICHELIN
© 2009 Michelin, Propriétaires-éditeurs
Société en commandite par actions au capital de 304 000 000 EUR.
R.C.S. Clermont-Fd B 855 200 507
Place des Carmes-Déchaux - 63 Clermont-Ferrand (France)
Imprimé en Italie - La Tipografica Varese - 21100 Varese
Made in France - DL : JANVIER 2010

CARTE STRADALI E TURISTICHE PUBBLICAZIONE PERIODICA
Reg. Trib. Di Milano N° 80 del 24/02/1997 Dir. Resp. FERRUCCIO ALONZI

While every effort is made to ensure that all information printed in this publication is corre
and up-to-date, Michelin accepts no liability for any direct, indirect or consequential losse
howsoever caused so far as such can be excluded by law.
Please help us to correct errors and omissions by writing to us at
MICHELIN Cartes et Guides - 46 avenue de Breteuil, 75324 PARIS cedex 07